I0435900

Exploring What It Effectively Means to Manage Carpal Tunnel Syndrome's

Physical, Social, and Emotional Crucibles
in a Return to Work Program

by

Dr. Stella Marie Rostkowski

authorHOUSE®

AuthorHouse™
1663 Liberty Drive
Bloomington, IN 47403
www.authorhouse.com
Phone: 1 (800) 839-8640

© 2016 Dr. Stella Marie Rostkowski. All rights reserved.

No part of this book may be reproduced, stored in a retrieval system, or transmitted by any means without the written permission of the author.

Published by AuthorHouse 12/17/2015

ISBN: 978-1-5049-6893-5 (sc)
ISBN: 978-1-5049-6890-4 (hc)
ISBN: 978-1-5049-6892-8 (e)

Library of Congress Control Number: 2015920842

Print information available on the last page.

Any people depicted in stock imagery provided by Thinkstock are models, and such images are being used for illustrative purposes only.
Certain stock imagery © Thinkstock.

This book is printed on acid-free paper.

Because of the dynamic nature of the Internet, any web addresses or links contained in this book may have changed since publication and may no longer be valid. The views expressed in this work are solely those of the author and do not necessarily reflect the views of the publisher, and the publisher hereby disclaims any responsibility for them.

This book is a work of non-fiction. Unless otherwise noted, the author and the publisher make no explicit guarantees as to the accuracy of the information contained in this book and in some cases, names of people and places have been altered to protect their privacy.

RAJ SINGH, PhD, Faculty Mentor and Chair
JENNIFER SCOTT, PhD, Committee Member
PHILLIP M. RANDALL, PhD, Committee Member

Barbara Butts Williams, PhD, Dean, School
of Business and Technology

A Dissertation Presented in Partial Fulfillment
Of the Requirements for the Degree
Doctor of Philosophy

Capella University
May 2015

TABLE OF CONTENTS

LIST OF TABLES

List of Figures

ABSTRACT

The purpose of this study was to identify why employees with carpal tunnel syndrome (CTS) do or do not complete their employer-sponsored Return to Work (RTW) program. Through the use of a constructivist grounded theory approach, which utilized semi-structured interviews, open-ended interviews, and observations, employees with CTS helped to reveal the essence of this disease. Data analysis in this study utilized the microanalysis techniques and procedures outlined by Strauss and Corbin, which consisted of open coding, axial coding, and selective coding. Study findings revealed five core categories, which showed the effects and the experiences of dealing with CTS physically, psychologically, psychosomatically, and sociologically. Within the five core categories, three to five subcategories showed the bi- and tri-directional relationships the effects of CTS have. These relationships were shown through the crossing and intertwined physical, sociological, and psychological behaviors that are depicted in the biosocial (BSP) model.

DEDICATION

In my lifetime, I have been fortunate enough to encounter several people whose words and actions have inspired me. I dedicate this dissertation to the early teachings of Miss Ewings, Mrs. Canepa, Mrs. Schaeffer, Miss Sanders, Mr. Guidace, and Mr. Curtain. Little did I realize at the time that your individual teachings and words of encouragement would be continuing inspiration and pinnacles in my life that would inspire me to help others.

I would also like to dedicate this dissertation to two very important people who entered my life when I was very young and passed away before they got the chance to see me mature into adulthood. To Mrs. Koziol, the only "mom" I ever knew and Mr. Pinsack, the only man I ever met that I would rank right up there with my dad. I love you both, and your presence is always in my heart.

Surprisingly, in my adult life, it was a complete stranger who inspired me to do this work through my experience with carpal tunnel syndrome. In 2006, I had to undergo nerve conduction test for my carpal tunnel syndrome and during this test I was asked by the nurse, "Is there anything else you can do with your life?" Little did I realize those words would echo in my head and become my crucible. I dedicate this dissertation and their findings to that nurse and all the employees with carpal tunnel syndrome. I hope the findings in this study help you find peace in your journey with this disease.

Last, but never least in my life, I dedicate this dissertation to my dad, the man who taught me how to wish upon a star and that I can do anything I set my mind to. I hope you know, Dad, you're my hero. I love you.

Acknowledgments

Thank you to all my friends and family who have supported me throughout this journey.

Thank you to my dissertation committee, Dr. Scott and Dr. Randall. I have enjoyed working with you both.

Special thanks to my mentor, Dr. Singh, whose words of encouragement and support even through some of the darkest points of my life helped keep me grounded and focused on making my dream to become a doctor come true.

CHAPTER 1

Introduction

Introduction to the Problem

In some organizations, Return to Work (RTW) programs are a benefit designed to slowly reintegrate the employees back into the workplace after they have been injured. Researchers have argued that these programs help build employees' confidence for being able to do their jobs after they have been injured (Schuhl & McMahon, 2006), while they also help employers reduce their Workers' Compensation costs (Centineo, 1986). However, research also showed that the "disabling impact of injuries" (Hunt, 2009, p. 2), goes far greater than the injury itself and needs to be examined on a more extensive and comprehensive level in order to understand why an employee succeeds or fails at completing their employer's RTW program when they have carpal tunnel syndrome (CTS). Current RTW programs are geared towards fixing one aspect of this disease, the physical.

However, research has shown that employees' feelings, emotions, and fears are not addressed, or even taken into account, in current RTW programs. Opsteegh et al. (2009) stated that personal effects can be "potential determinants" (p. 253) in RTW programs when the employers are working towards their own personal goals, rather than incorporating the needs of the employees into the program. Because of the organization's mandate to maintain a budget and pressure to eliminate employees with CTS due to the costs of their care, the employers could have a predetermined negative attitude towards CTS, employees with CTS, and RTWs geared toward employees with CTS.

Background of the Study

Current research on CTS considers the employees from either a case study perspective or a phenomenological perspective. Research has shown that case studies surrounding CTS centered on one of two aspects of the disease. First, a case study may concentrate on what CTS is and what the employees did in order to contract CTS (Atroshi, Lyren, & Gummeson, 2009; Giersiepen, & Spakkek, 2011; Hammond, & Harriss, 2012). The second approach involves measuring how fast the employees returned to work and how effective they were at their jobs once they returned (Baldwin & Butler, 2006; Butler, 2002; Fevre, Robinson, Lewis, & Jones, 2013). Phenomenological studies emphasized the employees' fear of the unknown and how they contended with their fear (Brotheridge & Lee, 2010; Cano, Leong, Heller, & Lutz, 2009; Cho, Zunin, Chao, Heiby, & Mckoy, 2012; Dae-seok, Gold, Kim, 2012). Research showed that employees' fears centralized around future employability prospects and meeting financial obligations (Brotheridge & Lee, 2010; He, Hu, Yu, Gu, & Liang, 2010; Jenkins, Watts, Duckworth, & McEachan, 2012; Koh, Moate, & Grinsell, 2009).

A comparison between case studies and phenomenological studies showed that both methodologies used people's experience to gather their data. This included conducting interviews with participants and utilizing journals. Research also showed (Baldwin & Butler, 2006; Butler, 2002; Fevre, Robinson, Lewis, & Jones, 2013; Kong & You, 2013; Kronstrom et al., 2011) that both study methodologies utilized *triangulation* as a means to validate the findings in a study. However, these two types of studies differed in the focal points of their recruitment and in how participants' experiences were used to generate data.

Case studies recruited participants for their studies because their physical experiences had similarities. Case studies asked the questions how and why in unstructured interviews in order to learn the specifics of how and why the situation occurred. Unstructured interviews allowed the participants' experience to drive the interview, rather than the researcher's interview driving the narrative of the participants' experience. Researchers utilized journals to document the participants' experience and to record specifics about participants' observations. Case studies do not adhere to a designated number of participants in order to conduct their studies (Dale et al., 2003; Stahl, Toomingas, Aborg, Ekberg, & Kjellberg, 2013).

Phenomenological studies used in-depth interviews so participants could reflect upon their personal experiences and the researcher could gain personal insight about the participants' feelings while they were going through the experience. Groenewald (2004) argued, "a person cannot reflect on lived experience while living through the experience" (p. 104). Gronewald (2004) stated that asking the participants to reflect upon their feelings as they were going through them changes the dynamic of the experience that the person is living through. In phenomenological studies, journals provide researchers with a written account of the participants' feelings. Phenomenological studies adhere to a prescribed number of participants, which is between 10 and 15 (Patton, 2002, p. 363).

Two notable differences between case studies and phenomenological studies are in their recruitment methods and their participation methods within the study (Groenwald, 2004; Patton, 2002). In phenomenological study, through a process known as "snowball sampling" (Groenwald, 2004, p. 9), researchers can recruit other participants into the study, based upon the recommendations from other study participants. In a phenomenological study, through a process known as bracketing, the researcher has the ability to interject their personal feelings into the study in order to help draw out the participant's experience.

Personal feelings were evident in research, which showed that CTS places stress on both the employee and the employer. Employee stress involves the employee's balancing a combination of multiple fears while trying to regain a semblance of their former life back (Dale et al., 2003). Multiple fears for the employee occur in a cycle, which starts and ends with the fear of job loss and also includes job satisfaction and future employment opportunities. Encompassed in the employee's fear circle is the impact that the job loss, loss of job satisfaction, and future employment opportunities will have on their private life (Dale et al., 2003).

Studies have also shown that employees who felt pressured into returning to work have sabotaged their employer's efforts in RTW programs in what is known as "worker comp return-to-work drama" (Butler, 2002, para. 6). According to Butler (2002), this is a direct "psychological impact" para. 17) imposed by CTS, because employees feel helpless against their injury. Employees are afraid to return to work, because they are afraid that their injury will return, and that their careers will end (Pransky, Benjamin, Hill-Fotouhi, Fletcher, & Himmelstein, 2002). The employees now associate their injury with their employer and their place of work. Employees inflicted with CTS encounter disease-inflicted limitations. As a direct result of these limitations, employees with CTS work twice as hard to prove their self-worth to their employers and co-workers (Brouwer et al., 2009; Côté & Coutu, 2010; Gravel et al., 2010; Heijbel, Josephson, Jensen, Stark, & Vingard, 2006). In the employees' minds, they have to prove to everyone, including themselves, that they can still do their jobs (Pransky et al., 2002).

Employers experience stress from a financial perspective. Research showed that CTS claims cost employers "over $4,000 per claim" (Faucett, Blanc, & Yelin, 2000, para. 4). Included in this cost is the hiring of temporary personnel to replace the injured worker while they are at home recuperating from their injury (Faucett et al., 2000). Research showed that employer bias against employees with CTS is due to its medically imposed restrictions (Faucett, Blanc, & Yelin, 2000; Vickers, 2009; Welch, Haile, Boden, & Hunting 2010), which are placed on the employee and to which the employer must adhere (Holmgren & Ivanoff, 2007). Holmgren and Ivanoff stated that the reason employers have this type of bias is because they feel trapped by the societal constraints of this disease, which state the employer has to allow the employee with CTS the right to work a reduced work schedule and find tasks that they can perform. In the employer's mind, this does not make good financial sense while trying to keep their budgets intact.

Statement of the Problem

The goal of current RTW programs is getting the employee back to work as quickly as possible, which meets the employer's physical and financial needs. However, past studies have shown that the emotional aspect plays a big part in CTS because employees fear job loss and meeting their financial obligations (Pransky et al., 2002). When these feelings are left to fester, the psychological effects of CTS produce physical effects in the employee with CTS, and the employee is left to treat the disease on his or her own.

Current research on CTS measures the employee from either a case study perspective or a phenomenological perspective (Pulvers & Hood, 2013; Stahl, Svensson, Petersson, & Ekberg, 2010; Stone, 2003; King, Tang, Yu, Luo, Liang, & He, 2011). Research showed that case studies surrounding CTS centered on one or two aspects of the disease. The first aspect focused on what CTS was and how the employee contracted it (Dale et al., 2003). The second aspect measured how long it took employees to return to work, assessed their job performance (Strunin & Boden, 2000; Stone, 2003), and focused on their fears (Pransky et al., 2002). Phenomenological studies also emphasized the employees' fear of the unknown (Faucett et al., 2000) and how they contended with it. Research showed that employees' fears centralized around future employability prospects (Pransky et al., 2002) and the ability to meet financial obligations (Viana, Sampaio, Mancini, Parreira, & Drummond, 2007).

MacEachen, Clarke, Franche, and Irvin (2006) argued that employers are concerned with reducing their Workers' Compensation costs because the typical insurance claim for CTS averaged "over $4,000 per claim" (Faucett et al., 2000, para. 4). Faucett et al. added that this figure did not include costs associated with hiring temporary work personnel to replace the employee. To combat their cost, employers took two different approaches. The first approach was to keep employees who are prone to CTS completely out of the work place through pre-employment screening, which subjected potential employees to a series of tests to determine if they would ever contract CTS (Evanoff & Kymes, 2010). However, several studies revealed employer bias when it came to pre-employment screening because the employer set the standards for acceptable test ranges (Dillenberger, 2009; Evanoff & Kymes, 2010; MacEachen et al., 2006; Wells, 2009). The second approach utilized RTW programs in the workplace for employees with CTS (MacEachen et al., 2006). However, the manager of the employee with CTS ran the RTW programs, and the results were subjected to what the manager deemed acceptable, including the employee's healing pace (Strunin & Boden, 2000).

Studies are deficient in this area because their findings are limited to either the employee or the employer. Research revealed that when an employee is diagnosed with CTS, he or she experiences a gamut of emotions (Waylett-Rendall & Niemeyer, 2004). In addition to dealing with the symptoms of CTS, employees are faced with the probability of having to change careers and still having to meet their financial obligations (Dale et al., 2003; Faucett et al., 2000). Previous studies also failed to discuss how the employees are treated by their co-workers when they return to work and how this affects their mindset towards their job, including any fears about their job security (Post, Krol, & Groothoff, 2005; Young, 2009b).

Research also revealed two resounding themes for employers: How can they reduce their Workers' Compensation cost? (Baldwin & Butler, 2006; Centineo, 1986; W. Young, 2009b) and how fast can employees return back to their jobs? The employees' abilities, physical and mental mindset, and limitations are not taken into account (Baldwin & Butler, 2006). Studies in this area also did not take into account employees' injuries returning. This is a psychological for employees (Faucett et al., 2000; Franche, Corbiere, Lee, Breslin, & Hepburn, 2007) and cost conducive for the employer (Baldwin & Butler, 2006). Dillenberger (2009) made the argument that RTW programs are designed with the mindset that one size fits all injuries (Dillenberger, 2009) and are usually led by managers who are not experienced in this area (W. Young, 2009b).

Purpose of the Study

The purpose of this grounded theory study was to discover how the physical, social, and emotional effects of carpal tunnel syndrome (CTS) affected employees' ability to complete an employer-sponsored Return to Work (RTW) program at their place of employment. Using a constructivist approach, relationships between employees, their manager, and their co-workers were examined. Personal needs in this study were demonstrated through the employees' morals, values, and ethics as they related to CTS and how the employees with CTS performed or did not perform in their employer-sponsored RTW program. The results found in these relationships will be compared to the business needs, healthcare needs, and personal needs by showing how they compared, contrasted, and coexisted with each other. Participants in this study consisted of 12 people who contracted CTS at work and participated in their employers' RTW programs.

Rationale

The data collection in this study was conducted in two phases that were specific to the employee and co-worker relationships and to the employee-employer relationship, in an attempt to identify idiosyncrasies that are specific to the participants being studied. Once the specific idiosyncrasies were identified, the remaining building blocks of why employees, employers, and co-workers act, react and feel the way they do towards CTS and RTW programs was uncovered through semi-structured interviews and participant observations. Findings from the semi-structured interviews and participant observations were deciphered through memoing, axial coding, and open coding in an attempt to look for reoccurring themes and identify the constructs that are generated by the data (Pandit, 1996).

Employee interviews and observations go more in depth to uncover the reasons employees felt the ways they did towards their injuries, and how they perceived their co-workers and employers felt about their being injured. The purpose of going deep into the employees' psyches was to get at the root of the problem in order to learn what they thought and felt about their injuries. Research has shown that part of their healing process is mental (Heijbel et al., 2006) for employees with CTS. Studies showed when the employees' psychological needs are met, employees will try to help themselves heal quicker (Heijbel et al., 2006). Studies also showed when the employees' psychological needs are neglected, employees take longer to return to their jobs (Heijbel et al., 2006) and will sabotage their employers' RTW program efforts (Butler, 2002, para. 6).

Open coding helped identify "concepts found in the data" (Pandit, 1996, p. 6). Axial coding was used to sort the employees' responses into five categories: (a) philosophical, (b) psychological, (c) sociological, (d) economical, and (e) employability. Specifics of how one category impacted the others and the rationale behind why one category impacted the others were noted. Selective coding w brought the findings of the different phases together in an attempt to generate a theory that was specific to employees. Reoccurring themes received pattern codes. The pattern codes were divided using selective coding to bring the findings of the compared phases together and generate a theory that was specific to the employees' co-workers.

Selected coding findings and the visual diagram formed the avowal for the "within case analysis" (Creswell, 2009, p. 75) findings. Resulting data from observational definitions and unit analysis answered the research questions, because they filled in the research gap left from case studies and phenomenological studies, which minimally measured aspects of CTS. The gap in research consisted of the remaining areas of study that have not been conducted and combined together to depict an overall, encompassing picture of CTS, including its effects and the human experience in the workplace.

Research revealed when employees are diagnosed with CTS, they experience a gamut of emotions (Waylett-Rendall & Niemeyer, 2004). In addition to dealing with the symptoms of CTS, the employees face the probability of having to change careers and the responsibility of continuing to meet their financial obligations (Dale et al., 2003; Faucett et al., 2000). However, what has not been studied was how the employees were treated by their co-workers when they returned to work and how this affected the employees' mindset towards their jobs and their fears about job security (Post et al., 2005; Young, 2004). Through a constructivist grounded theory approach, the examination of the relationships between employees, their managers, and their co-workers showed how actions guide reactions in RTW programs. Once the actions and reactions were identified, insight into the determinants of why an employee does or does not complete the employer sponsored RTW program were revealed.

Research Questions

RQ1. How does an employee afflicted with carpal tunnel syndrome's morals, values, and ethics dictate his or her success or failure rate for completing a RTW program?

RQ2. How much impact does an injured employee's psychological makeup have on how well he or she will perform at his or her job after returning from a workplace injury?

RQ3. How do the effects of employer's bias towards employees with CTS affect the employee's successful completion rate of a RTW program?

RQ4. How does an employer's morals, values, and ethics dictate whether he or she will implement a RTW program for employees inflicted with CTS?

RQ5. How do co-workers psychologically affect an employee with CTS's completion rate in an employer-sponsored RTW Program?

Significance of the Study

The significance of this study was to fill in the gap in research, which was identified in previous studies done on RTW programs that concentrated on CTS. Prior research by Waylett-Rendall and Niemeyer in 2004 revealed that in order to "identify emerging patterns and predicative relationships" (p. 50) of CTS, its "dichotomy needs to be studied as a whole" (p. 50). He, Hu, Yu, Gu, and Liang (2010) stated that identifying "potential determinants would be helpful in improving RTW rate and minimizing the duration of absenteeism following an injury" (p. 378).

Dale et al. (2003) made the argument that in order to learn more about the CTS experience, people need to be interviewed individually and feel safe when discussing the effects of their disease. Berger, Vermeulen, Koelman, van Schaik, and Roos (2012) stated that part of the effect of CTS is its social aspect, and before implementing a RTW program, employers need to take "into account the specific characteristics of the population, as well as the social, political and cultural context in which the program will be implemented and used" (p. 321). Current studies only measured one to two aspects of CTS and how it affected either the employees or the employers. The gap in research is the other remaining areas of the study that have not been conducted and combined together in order to depict an overall, encompassing picture of the disease, which includes its effects and the human experience in the workplace.

According to Hunt (2009), the "disabling impact of injuries" (p. 2) is far greater than the injury itself and needs to be examined on a more extensive and comprehensive level in order to understand why an injured employee succeeds or fails at completing their employer's RTW program. The employees' experience as a whole, their surroundings, their co-workers, and their employer must be physically viewed and examined in order to establish patterns that showed how actions, which are morals, values, and ethics, guided employees', their co-workers', and their employers' reactions in a RTW program geared for reintroducing employees with CTS back into the work place. How people dealt with CTS is where the differences occur. This is the aspect of this disease that has not been studied: why people act, react, and feel the way they do.

Past studies have shown that many of the effects of CTS are emotional because employees fear job loss and failure to meet financial obligations (Pransky et al., 2002; Viana et al., 2007). When these feelings are left to fester, the psychological effects of CTS caused physical symptoms in the employees with CTS. With this missing information, employers can tailor RTW programs that are specific to the employees' needs. By doing this, employers are helping to ease employees' fears about coming back to work and about getting re-injured (Faucett et al., 2000; Murphy & Rosenblum, 2006; Pransky et al., 2002).

Additionally, by tailoring a RTW program to its employees, the employer will have to spend less on temporary personnel and work re-assignments, because the employees' psychological need of having their organization care about their health and well-being is reinforced (Heijbel et al., 2006; MacEachen et al., 2006). Research showed that part of the employees' healing process is mental (Heijbel et al., 2006). Heijbel et al.'s study showed that when the employees' psychological needs are met, they will try to help themselves heal quicker and conversely, when employees' psychological needs re neglected, they will take longer to return to their jobs. Murphy and Rosenblum (2006) argued that when a psychological feeling exacerbates in the employees' minds, it is because the employees' environment allotted the opportunity for it to build and fester. A further benefit of tailoring a RTW program to the employees' needs is physically showing how co-workers and employers worked together towards the common goal of helping return the employee back to work as quickly as possible. This can aid in removing hostility, resentment, and feelings of favoritism and jealously within the workplace and amongst co-workers (Strunin & Boden, 2000).

Definition of Terms

At this stage in the research, the physical, social, and emotional effects of CTS will generally be defined as (a) physical: "involving or requiring bodily contact" ("Physical," 2013); (b) social: "of, relating to, or characteristic of the experience, behavior, and interaction of persons forming groups: ("Social," 2013); and (c) emotional: "actuated, effected, or determined by emotion rather than reason" ("Emotional," 2013).

Biopsychosocial (BPS) Model. "States that biological, psychological, and social factors are involved in the causes and manifestation of health and disease" (Boundless, 2014, para. 1).

Ergonomics. Comprised of two Greek words, *ergon*, meaning *work* (Banham, 1994, para.1), and *nomos*, which means *laws* (Human Factors & Ergonomics Society 2010, para. 2). The official definition adopted in 2000 by the International Ergonomics Association (IEA; 2015) was utilized in this dissertation:

> Ergonomics (or human factors) is the scientific discipline concerned with the understanding of interactions among humans and other elements of a system, and the profession that applies theory, principals, data and methods to design in order to optimize human well-being and overall system performance. (para.1)

Ethics. "A set of moral principles, often ones relating to specified groups, field, or form of conduct, that guide an individual's or group behavior" (Julnes & Bustelo, 2014, p. 526).

Kantianism.

> Derived from or analogous to a position of Immanuel Kant, esp. his doctrines that there are synthetic a priori propositions which order our experience but are not derived from it, that metaphysical conclusions can be inferred from the nature of possible experience, that duty is to be done for its own sake and not as a means to any other end, and that there is a world of things-in-themselves to be distinguished from mere phenomena. ("Kantianism," 2015, para.1)

Morals. Velasquez (2006) stated morals come from morality, which is the standard that an individual or a group has about what, is right and wrong or good and evil.

Values. "Represent beliefs or ideals shared by the members of a culture about what is good or desirable in a pluralistic world" (Julnes & Bustelo, 2014, p. 525).

Workplace Bullying.

A situation in which one or several individuals persistently, and over a period of time, perceive themselves as being on the receiving end of negative actions from superiors or coworkers, and where the target of the bullying finds it difficult to defend him or herself against these actions. (Nielsen & Einarsen, 2012, p. 309)

Assumptions and Limitations

Theoretical assumptions associated with the constructivist grounded theory are (a) in constructivist grounded theory, data is generated by the participants' stories or the participant's experience (Creswell, 2009; Ghezeljeh & Emami, 2009; Mills, Bonner, & Francis, 2006). One assumption was that the participants in this study would be honest with the details of their experience; (b) another assumption was that the theory would "explain how a phenomenon is being addressed/solved/managed" (Hamilton, 2011, p. 11); (c) another assumption was that the theory would be modifiable based on new findings in the study (Hamilton, 2011, p. 11); (d) the theory was generated based on assumptions participants bring into their work (Levy, 2006). According to Crotty (1998), people bring their thoughts and beliefs about a situation into their work. For example, if a person feels they are being harassed by a co-worker, then their actions and reactions to the co-worker will be different than their response to another co-worker who is not harassing them. According to Guba and Lincoln (1989), constructivism is a research paradigm that denies the existence of an objective reality, asserting instead that realities are social constructions of the mind, and that "there exist as many such constructions as there are individuals" (p. 2). Based upon this statement, another assumption was that this study would uncover different and multiple "social constructions of the mind" (Guba & Lincoln, 1989, p. 2) and the meaning implicit in the data would be uncovered (Mills et al., 2006); (e) "further data collection (or sampling) is based on emerging concepts" (Egan, Bambra, Petticrew, & Whitehead, 2009, p. 278). Another assumption was that concepts would emerge from the collected data provided by the participants in this study, and data analysis would be done by a continuous cycle of comparing (Egan, 2009; Guba & Lincoln, 1989; Hamilton, 2011; Levy, n.d.; Mills et al., 2006); and (f) the study incorporated the assumption that the collected data could be continuously compared.

Topical assumptions associated with constructivist grounded theory are (a)"concepts derived from literature may provide a source for comparing data at a dimensional level" (Levy, 2006, p. 11); (b) literature provides insight (Levy, 2006, p. 11); (c) "literature can also be used to confirm findings and determine situations where the literature may be incorrect, over simplistic and only partially explaining the phenomena" (Levy, 2006, p. 11); (d) current research on the topic of the study will be applicable in this study (Egan, 2009); and (e) "literature is able to provide examples of similar phenomena that can stimulate our thinking about properties or dimensions that we can then use to examine the data in front of us" (Mills et al., 2006, p. 5).

Methodological assumptions associated with the constructivist ground theory are (a) data was generated by the participants' stories, which are also referred to as the participant's experience (Creswell, 2009; Ghezeljeh & Emami, 2009; Mills et al., 2006); (b) meaning will be found in the data that is uncovered (Mills et al., 2006). According to Egan (2009), constructivist grounded theory seeks to define "meaning in the data, searching for, and questioning tacit meanings about values, beliefs and ideologies" (p. 278); and (c) "further data collection (or sampling) is based on emerging concepts" (Egan, 2009, p. 278).

Theoretical/Conceptual Framework

The conceptual theoretical framework for this study focused on the "interrelationships" (Miles & Huberman, 1994, p. 19) between the employees with CTS, their co-workers, and their managers. A conceptual diagram was utilized to show how the injured employees' fears could affect their behavior at work. Focusing on the effects that interrelationships have in the workplace drew a connection to the missing link between the psychological and physical effects of CTS.

This study was grounded in the field of organization and management, because it dealt with two dilemmas within the workplace. The first dilemma was the employee with CTS. The second dilemma was how co-workers and employers react to working with someone who has CTS. When an employee is diagnosed with CTS, research revealed employees experienced a gamut of emotions (Waylett-Rendall

& Niemeyer, 2004). In addition to dealing with the symptoms of CTS, the employee was also faced with the probability of having to change careers and still meet their financial obligations (Dale et al., 2003; Faucett et al, 2000). Shaw, Robertson, Pransky, and McLellan (2003) stated, "Work provides structure to an individual's life" (p. 246). Viana et al (2007) furthered Shaw et al.'s (2003) argument when they stated that people begin to wonder how they will meet their financial obligations and basic needs when the foundation of their life is taken away. Pransky et al. (2002) stated that when employees' foundation is weakened by injury and compounded by the psychological realization their career is fading, the employees may eventually crumble under the pressure.

Research also showed the average medical cost associated with a Workers' Compensation claim for CTS is "over $4,000 per claim" (Faucett et al., 2000, para. 4). Faucett et al. also argued that in addition to paying the Workers' Compensation Claim, employers still have the additional cost associated with hiring temporary workers to fill in for the employee while they are healing. This study fills in the gap of previous studies conducted on RTW programs that focused on CTS, because those studies measured only one or two aspects of the disease and only showed how CTS affected either the employee or the employer. The gap in research was the other remaining areas of studies that were not considered and combined in order to depict an overall, encompassing picture of the disease, which included its effects and the human experience in the workplace.

Through the use of a constructivist grounded theory approach, relationships between employees, their manager, and their co-workers were examined to identify the determinants of why an employee did or did not complete the employer sponsored RTW program. The results found in these relationships were compared to the business needs, healthcare needs, and personal needs, by showing how they compared, contrasted, and co-existed with each other. With this missing information, employers could begin tailoring RTW programs that are specific to the employees' needs. By doing this, employers could help to ease the fears that employees may be experiencing about coming back to work and about getting re-injured (Faucett et al., 2000; Murphy & Rosenblum, 2006; Pransky et al., 2002). Additionally, by tailoring a RTW program to the employees, the employers will have to spend less on temporary personnel and work re-assignments, because the employees' psychological need of their organization caring about their health and well-being is being reinforced (Heijbel et al., 2006; MacEachen et al., 2006), and they are likely to return to work sooner (Heijbel et al., 2006).

Research showed that part of the injured employees' healing process is mental, and when the employees' psychological needs are met, they will try to help themselves heal quicker. Heijbel et al. (2006) also asserted that when the employees' psychological needs are neglected, they take longer to return to their jobs. Additional studies showed that this type of psychological feeling became exacerbated in the employees' minds and when it was allowed to fester (Murphy & Rosenblum, 2006). Further benefits of tailoring a RTW program to the employees' needs included showing how employers worked with the injured employees towards the common goal of helping the employees with CTS return to work as quickly as possible. Strunin and Boden (2000) argued that this illustrative element could aid in removing hostility, resentment, and feelings of favoritism and jealously within the workplace and amongst co-workers.

Organization of the Remainder of the Study

Chapter 2 will consist of the literature review, which discusses studies from the employer's and the employees' perspective of this disease. The primary focus found in studies from an employer's perspective centralized on the theme of employers keeping their Workers' Compensation cost down and the methods they chose to accomplish this. Studies from the employees' perspective focused on the physical, emotional, psychological, and financial strangulation this disease imposes. Chapter 3 will reiterate the purpose of the study and explain in detail the specifics of the study, such as its design, research sample, how data was collected, and the significance of collecting data in this manner. Chapter 4 will discuss the findings from the study. Chapter 5 will discuss the implications and recommendations from the findings.

CHAPTER 2

Literature Review

Introduction

Musculoskeletal disorders affect an estimated 1.8 million workers (Drutman, 2004, para. 1). Because of the number of workers affected, in 1996, OSHA attempted to implement an ergonomic law, which forced employers to customize an employee's workstation to their exact measurements. Because of the cost involved, the Congressional Review Act of 1996 was used to veto OSHA's proposed ergonomic bill. Because of the combination of the stipulations in the Congressional Review Act and OSHA's being a government-regulated entity lawmakers are now unable to propose a bill that is similar to the one that was vetoed. OSHA responded with a "4-pronged approach" (Nash, 2002, para. 1), which stated that ergonomic policies and procedures are implemented on a voluntary basis per "industry" (para. 1). Because there is no one-size-fits-all to ergonomics, most employers do not have ergonomic policies and procedures in place.

In 2008, there were 1,078,100 reported cases of CTS in the workplace (Hepburn, Franche, & Francis, 2010). Literature showed that CTS is now arguably the "most common entrapment neuropathy and repetitive trauma disorder" (Ghasemi, Rezaee, Chavoshi, Mojtahed, & Koushki, 2012, p. 1). However, "despite worldwide attention for more than four decades, musculoskeletal disorders (MSDs) remain a substantial concern at work and result in considerable personal and societal burden" (Wells, 2009, p. 117). The societal burden of CTS and the discrimination against employees with CTS have been well documented and shown to be prevalent in workplaces today. Studies revealed that employers have gotten more sophisticated in their discrimination tactics, and their tactics are deemed socially acceptable because there are no laws that state otherwise (Egan, Bambra, Petticrew, & Whitehead, 2009; Einarsen, Hoel, Zapf, & Cooper, 2011).

When an employee is injured at work, there are certain policies, procedures, and protocols that are supposed to be followed. However, because of the lack set regulations for return to work programs (RTW), most organizations deem this as another inconvenience associated with this disease and employ various sabotage methods to thwart the employees' progress in the RTW. Studies showed that this was accomplished through bullying, demoting the employee with CTS, and various humiliation tactics, which increased with intensity over time, such as gossiping, spreading rumors, and mobbing in order for organizations to rid themselves of this inconvenience.

This literature review will discuss the various examples of employer discrimination and how they are rooted in societal influence, which will show the lengths society is willing to go to in order to maintain its own sense of well-being in the workplace. In order to fully depict the effects of these actions, it is necessary to provide an explanation of the negative effects on the employee with CTS, physical, social, and mental well-being, along with the negative effects and consequences these actions have on organizations and other employees. While some injured employees have demonstrated that their injury can serve as a double-edged sword to their employer, studies revealed that the majority of employees with CTS do want to return to work and continue to be productive members of society. Because of the different tactics and coping mechanisms discussed, individual recommendations are made at the end of each section with the aim of removing the negativity from the workplace and creating a functional, cohesive workplace.

Employers' Perspectives

Financial

The purpose of this section of the literature review is to show that the effects of CTS affect more than the employee inflicted with the disease. However, literature surrounding management's perspective about employees with CTS and managing employees with CTS was very limited in its focus and concentrated on the financial implication this disease has for employers. However, numerous studies discussed the financial inconvenience and disruption that CTS has in the workplace for employers, along with societal influence and implications, which showed how deeply entrenched the negative activity was imbedded into the workplace culture.

The financial inconveniences noted by employers included the cost associated with the Workers Compensation claims for the employees with CTS (Theberge & Neumann, 2013) and having to hire temporary workers, who have to be trained to do the injured employee's job (May, Li, Mencl, & Huang, 2013). Opsteegh et al. (2009) argued that the financial implications, inconveniences, and disruptions brought on by having an employee with CTS in the workplace directly related to the employer's being predisposed to bias against employees with this disease.

Research showed that the predisposition that employers exhibit against employees with CTS are not personal, meaning the employers do not dislike the employees. Rather, the predisposition started with the financial burden of CTS on employers, and management uses the prejudice as a motivating factor to keep the costs down. In fact, CTS claims cost employers "over $4,000 per claim" (Theberge & Neumann, 2013). However, studies also showed a "negative effect on health and risk factors" (Koukoulaki, 2013, p. 198) on co-workers when employers attempted to avoid hiring temporary personnel and run a leaner production base.

Multiple studies made the argument that because employees spend a good portion of their day at work, any negativity caused by work will eventually manifest itself in symptoms that are felt mentally and exhibited physically in the employee (Gilbreath, 2012; Hasselberg, Jonsdottir, Ellbin, & Skagert, 2014; Nixon, Mazzola, Bauer, Kruger, & Spector, 2011). Mental and physical symptoms directly linked to workplace stress included "gastrointestinal problems and sleep disorders" (Nixon et al., 2011, p. 1), panic attacks (Shoss & Shoss, 2012), increased musculoskeletal injuries (Koukoulaki, 2013; Melin & Harriss, 2010), depression (Koukoulaki, 2013), exhaustion (Hasselberg et al., 2014), anger, frustration, increased sick days (Jacobsen et al., 2014), and higher employee turnover because employees quit from being forced to work longer hours over an extensive time frame (Koukoulaki, 2010; Melin & Harriss, 2010). Because of the continual downward spiral of mental and physical effects, employers were forced to look at other means to maintain their bottom line.

The spiral of mental and physical CTS effects produced two types of employers; ones who wanted to fix the problem and ones who wanted to eliminate the problem. Employers who wanted to fix the problem utilized work redesign methodology in an attempt to help stabilize the employee with CTS's mental and physical well-being. This task was accomplished through return to work (RTW) programs. The employers who wanted to eliminate the problem from their workplace used whatever tactics were necessary to prevent and eliminate CTS influences and burdens from their workplaces. This task was accomplished through pre-employment screening and workplace bullying.

Return to Work Programs

Return to work (RTW) programs entered the United States workforce in the 1990s as a multifaceted approach and solution to combating employers' rising Workers Compensation Cost for CTS (Ahlstrom, Hagberg, & Dellve, 2013; Carroll, Rick, Pilgrm, Cameron, & Hillage, 2010; Iles, Wyatt, & Prasky, 2012; Shiri et al., 2011), having to hire temporary personnel, production loss, build an employee's confidence, and reduce their stress and anxiety about performing at their job after they have been injured (Carroll et al., 2010; Huijs, Koppes, Taris, & Blonk, 2012; Iles et al., 2012; Netterstrom, Frieble, & Ladegaard, 2013; Rubin, 2013; Schuhl & McMahon, 2006). However, research revealed that implementing and integrating this multifaceted approach into the workplace was harder that it appeared.

There are no laws, rules, regulations, or standards for setting up an RTW program in the workplace, and minimal literature exists on designing an RTW program for employees with CTS. Additionally, unless an employer had an "occupational employment staff" (Wrapson & Mewse, 2011, p. 1,728), the employer was able to set the standards of what was deemed acceptable and unacceptable in the RTW program, thereby having "an important influence in return to work outcomes" (p. 1,728). For example, if an employee with CTS is placed on a reduced work-hour schedule for a fixed number of weeks by their doctor and the employee normally works a 40-hour workweek, the employer still wanting their productivity to remain intact can give the employee with the reduced work-hour schedule more work than they can physically complete. When the employee fails to complete their work because they are not medically allowed to, the employer can claim that the employee with CTS is no longer capable of performing the job they were originally hired to do (Anderson, Neielsen, & Brinkmann, 2012; Wrapson & Mewse, 2011; A. E. Young, 2009; W. Young, 2009) and may terminate the employee's employment. Research showed while this was unethical, it is secretly deemed acceptable in the workplace (Cornelius, van der Klink, Groothoff, & Brouwer, 2011; A. E. Young, 2009) and has gone on for years (Eakin, 2010; Schur, Kruse, Blasi, & Blank, 2009). Research showed that employees with CTS have difficulty being rehired once they have left their positions and "typically earn an average of 27% less than prior to their injury" (Eakin, 2010, p. 119).

No statistical or literary evidence supported the claim that RTWs reduce an employer's Workers Compensation insurance cost. Some evidence indicated that employees did return to work faster because of being in the RTW (Baldwin & Bulter, 2006; Carroll et al., 2010; Hammond & Harriss, 2012). However, only a smattering of these studies exist. Most studies surrounding this area showed that employers were looking for a quick fix (He et al., 2010; Heijble et al., 2006; Hoefsmit, de Rijk, & Houkes, 2013; Idris, Dollard, & Yulita, 2014) to their problem and did not want to exert the effort it would take to implement or integrate the RTW into their workplace.

Research also showed that in order for a RTW program to be effective in the workplace, it has to be established quickly (Ammendolia, et al, 2009; Pomaki, Franche, Murray, Khushrushahi, & Lampinen, 2011) in order to reduce the psychological effects of CTS. Research also showed that there has to be a strong partnership between an ergonomist, a psychologist, and the organization where the employee with CTS works, including physical and social support from management and co-workers (Murad, O'Brien, Farnworth, & Chien, 2013), along with a mutual trust and respect between the employee with CTS and management (Ammendolia, et al, 2009; Hoefsmit et al., 2013; W. Kong et al., 2012; Stahl, Svensson, Petersson, & Ekberg, 2010;Wainwright, Wainwright, Keogh, & Eccleston, 2013). Studies further showed that employees with CTS would not return to their jobs if they did not feel safe (Ahlstrom et al., 2012; Cornelius et al., 2011; Pomaki et al., 2011). Studies also showed that employers would not consider implementing a RTW program for employees with CTS if they did not feel they could trust the employee (Stahl et al., 2010; Wainwright et al., 2013; Wynne-Jones et al., 2011) because of their exhibited behavior prior to their injury (Wainwright et al., 2013, p. 501). This mistrust might stem from excessive absenteeism, lack of commitment to their job, and poor work ethic (Stahl et al., 2010, Wynne-Jones et al., 2011).

RTW Programs and Social Structure

Employees experience a strong need to be accepted at work, because work provides social structure. Kirsh, Slack, and King (2012) and Kronstrom et al. (2011) argued that the importance of human interaction and social organizational acceptance in the workplace had a direct link on employees' mental and physical health, Kirsh et al. (2012) furthered Kronstrom et al.'s (2011) argument when they stated that employees with CTS experience "a loss of identity" (Kirsh et al., 2012, p. 235) when work is forcibly taken away. It is the "loss of identity" that causes employees with CTS to have an internal, psychological panic attack (Kronstrom et al, 2011; Riach & Loretto, 2009). Riach and Loretto (2009) and Roscigno, Hodson, and Lopez (2009a) argued that when employees with CTS is socially accepted, they are able to focus and concentrate on doing their job. However, when an employee with CTS is socially ostracized at work, the employees' "behavior is the product of thoughts related to an activating event" (Roscigno, Hodson, & Lopez, 2009b, p. 729). The "activating event" (p. 729), in this instance, is the employee's loosing social grace at work. Thus, the employees with CTS concentrate all their efforts on regaining their social organizational acceptance in the workplace and less time and effort on doing their job (Roscigno et al., 2009b).

Because of this phenomenon, Riach and Loretto (2009) argued that employees with CTS's productivity decreased significantly, their employer lost trust in them, and other workers noticed their lack of productivity. Roscigno et al. (2009b) argued these trends lead to gossiping, rumors, and questions arising about the employees' future within the organization. All of these events can trigger another activating event for the employees with CTS and cause them to modify their behavior from gaining social grace and acceptance to outwardly promoting their self-worth in their organization. Research showed over extended periods of time that repeated activating events caused employees with CTS to experience high levels of stress, anxiety, and hopelessness because they were unable to concentrate their efforts solely on one thing during their day. The psychological effects of the activating events eventually manifested themselves into physical symptoms (Persson, Bernfort, Wahlin, Oberg, & Ekberg, 2014; Sullivan, Adams, & Ellis, 2013) for employees' with CTS.

The physical symptoms affected the employees' sleep (Lallukka, Haaramo, Rahkonen, & Sivertsen, 2013; Salo et al., 2010), and sleep deprivation has been shown to increase and intensify the effects of stress, anxiety, hopelessness, and increase the number of sick days (Idris et al., 2014; Lallukka et al., 2013; Salo et al., 2010) These effects are caused primarily by the psychological and physical exhaustion the body feels from constantly being stressed and not having the opportunity to disengage from the stress (Jacobsen et al., 2014; Lallukka et al., 2013; Mug Kang, Young, & Kim, 2011; Salo et al., 2010). Studies showed that the effects from "activating events" (Roscigno et al., 2009b, p. 729) eventually crept into every facet of the employees with CTS's personal lives (Kronstrom et al., 2011; Mug Kang et al., 2011), which caused employees with CTS to experience additional activating events, which increased the employees' sick days, reduced their productivity even further, and caused additional work stress. The strain of the psychological weight of the constant continuum of spiraling activating events eventually crippled and exhausted employees psychologically to a point where they were unable to perform at work and function at home. Feeling helpless against their injuries, employees with CTS quit their jobs (Knauf, Schultz, Stewart, Gatchel, 2014; Sullivan et al., 2013) and attempt to regain some form of normalcy in their lives. Research showed that it could take employees with CTS months or years to recover from this experience (W. Kong et al., 2012; Kronstrom et al., 2011; MacIntosh, 2012; Martin & Martin, 2010; McFarlane, 2013).

Societal Influence

Societal induced pressures of keeping budgets intact, and minimalizing the appearance of CTS in the workplace in an attempt to maintain the "social model of disability" (Fevre, Robinson, Lewis, & Jones, 2013, p. 288) resulted in the magnification of the predisposition that employers have towards employees with CTS (Opsteegh et al., 2009). Research showed that there was a significant financial commitment from the employer to implement a RTW program into the workplace (Knauf et al., 2014; Stahl, Toomingas, Aborg, Ekbreg, & Kjellberg, 2013), which included paying overtime to employees for working additional hours and hiring an Occupational Rehabilitation specialist. In instances where employees were unable to return to their original positions because of their injury, the employer viewed this as a negative and counter-productive, because in addition to having to retrain, or transfer the employee to do another job, the employer had to permanently replace the employee with CTS and train a new employee. In the employer's mind, the amount of time and effort required to assist one inured employee, versus hiring a new employee was more than they were willing to commit to. Because there was not a significant financial increase and productivity decreased due to the additional effort required by co-workers working additional hours, most employers abandoned their RTW programs before fully giving them a chance to produce the outcome they were looking to achieve.

Multiple studies by Opsteegh et al. (2009), Fevre et al. (2013), Samnani and Singh, (2012), and Wheeler, Halbesleben, and Shanine (2010) argued that because of the pressure employers received from societal influence, employers indirectly work against employees with CTS's healing processes and concentrate their effort towards eliminating employees with CTS from their organizations. Societal influences discussed the lengths employers were willing to take in order to avoid having CTS in their workplace, which included pre-employment screening and bullying.

Pre-employment Screening

Evanoff and Kymes (2010) conducted pre-employment screening in 2009 using the Markov model for a period of one year to depict the "probability that someone would develop CTS, continue working without developing CTS, and leave work due to other reasons than CTS" (p. 2). The Markov model "is a mathematical method for estimating the costs and consequences of events that repeat in a cyclical manner with each set of iterations referred to as a Markov cycle" (Evanoff & Kymes, 2010, p. 3). Participants in this study were selected from the unidentified organization's employment applications. "Total claim cost to the employer or employer's insurer for a case of Carpal Tunnel Syndrome in the USA, including direct medical and disability cost" (Evanoff & Kymes, 2010, p. 2) were represented in this study by published workers compensation claims. The results of Evanoff and Kymes's study showed that the unidentified employer was able to reduce its worker compensation claims by 32% by pre-employment screening for CTS. Over the course of five years, "3,279 workers were rejected for employment" (p. 3).

Additional studies regarding pre-employment screening for CTS showed that when employers used pre-employment screening for CTS, their cost increased $300 dollars per employee, because of the added cost to screen the employee (Lewis, Mauffrey, Newman, Lambert, & Hull, 2009). Additional studies also revealed that there was "low quality evidence that pre-employment examinations that were specific to certain jobs or health problems could reduce occupational disease, injury, or sickness absence" (Lewis et al., 2009, p. 84). Because of the conflicting results found in these studies, further research is recommended to determine, which study has stronger evidence on the financial benefits or determents of per employment screening.

Bullying

Research revealed that workplace bullying is not a new concept, but rather one that has been kept quiet in the workplace and serves as a way to cause "severe social, psychological, and psychosomatic problems" (Einarsen, Hoel, Zapf, & Cooper, 2011, p. 4) for the person being targeted. Research showed that the implied, intended outcome was to eliminate the employee with CTS from the workplace through whatever means possible (Einarsen, Hoel, & Notelaers, 2009; Sloan et al., 2010; Rugulies, 2012), which included both physical and mental harassment (Devonish, 2013; Glasø, Vie, Holmadal, & Einarsen, 2011) of the person being targeted, social exclusion (Appelbaum, Semerjian, & Mohan, 2012; Fevre et al., 2013), and "verbal abuse, accusations, and public humiliation" (Hauge, Skogstad, & Einarsen, 2010, p. 427). Research showed if the employee being targeted did not conform to what was deemed the acceptable "social order" (Murray, 2013, p. 112) within the organization, bullying efforts were increased to the extent that the employee being targeted experienced severe mental stress and anguish (Bailien, De Cuyper, & De Witte, 2011; Dae-seok, Gold, & Kim, 2012; Rodriguez-Munoz, Baillien, De-Witte, Moreno-Jimenez, & Pastor, 2009; Nielsen, Hetland, Matthiesen, & Einarsen, 2012; Selenko, & Batinic, 2013), "moral stress" (Murray, 2013, p. 113), increased sick days (O'Reilly & Aquino, 2011), loss of job satisfaction and security (Finne, Knardalh, & Lau, 2011; Houshmand, O'Reilly, Robinson, & Wolff, 2012; McCormack, Casimir, Djurkovic, & Yang, 2009; O'Reilly & Aquino, 2011), and they eventually left the workplace (Berthelsen, Skogstad, Lau, & Einarsen, 2011; D'Cruz & Noronha, 2010; Hogh, Hoel, & Carneiro, 2011).

Hierarchal Bullying

Hierarchal bullying in the workplace is not a new concept; it is an "abuse of power" (Schumann, Craig, & Rosu, 2014, p. 846), which is directly aimed at forcing the employer's will onto the employee by getting the employee to submit to what the employer wanted through psychological mind control and manipulation (D'Cruz & Noronha, 2010; De Cuyper, Baillien, & De Witte, 2009; Einarsen et al., 2009; Einarsen et al., 2011; Finne et al., 2011; Schumann et al., 2014). Hierarchal bullying "encapsulates a series of systematically negative acts that derive into social, psychological, and psychosomatic problems for the victim" (Montes, Muniz, Leal-Rodrguez, & Leal-Millan, 2014, p. 2659). Research showed that employer bullying starts with the first bullying action of public and private humiliation (Finne et al., 2011; Gumbus & Lyons, 2011; Hauge et al., 2010). Once the employer had successfully humiliated the employee, efforts were increased to sabotage the employee's work and discredit the employee with co-workers (Hoefsmit et al., 2013; Hogh et al., 2011; Idris et al., 2014; Law et al., 2011).

Public and private humiliation begin with employers degrading the employee at work in front of other co-workers and colleagues in order to discredit the employee in front of their co-workers and make them uncomfortable around the employee (Agervold, 2009; Idris et al., 2014; Law et al., 2011). This enables the employer to isolate the employee (Armstrong, 2011; Atkinson, 2014; Baillien et al., 2011) and prevent them from gaining support or sympathy from their co-workers (Baillien et al., 2011), which could later be used to sabotage the bullying managers' efforts.

Several studies showed that employers sabotage employees' work by interfering in its progress (Agervold, 2009; Roscigno et al., 2009a), being overly critical of the work (Atkinson, 2014; Roscigno et al., 2009a; Rugulies, 2012), and giving the employee an assignment that they know the employee will not finish on time (Roscigno et al., 2009a; Selenko & Batinic, 2013). The employer does this in order to create and show a pattern of the employees' work performance, which can be used to maintain control over the employee through denying vacation, or sick days, promotions, or allowing the employee to transfer to another department (Selenko & Batinic, 2013; Sloan, Matyiok, Schmitz, & Short, 2010). Studies showed denying employee transfers to other departments was one of the severest of manipulations and bullying tactics on the employers part because it invoked helplessness, desperation, and made the employee feel that they had no control over the situation. Research showed that the employee felt hopeless and stuck in their position (Sloan et al., 2010; Stojanova, 2014; Tracy, Lutgen-Sandvik, & Alberts, 2006; Vie, Glasø, & Einarsen, 2010; Wheeler et al., 2010).

Managers have also sabotaged an employee's work efforts in order to discredit the employee with their co-workers (Idris et al., 2014; Law et al., 2011). The manager starts by talking behind the employee's back to other co-workers about the employee's performance and uses key buzz words or phrases to invoke a negative response from the employee's co-workers. Research showed that this sabotage removes any chance of the employee gaining support or sympathy from their co-workers when the bullying intensifies (Idris et al., 2014; Law et al., 2011; Vickers, 2009; Wiedmer. 2011).

Studies showed that hierarchal bullying exists in the workplace today, because this type of management style has been engrained into the organizational culture and is now accepted as the norm (Roscigno et al., 2009b; Vickers, 2009). Employees who are bullied at work by their managers are often isolated, because other employees fear the same reprimand or fate from management and engage in the bullying efforts in order to avoid being victimized as well (Agervold, 2009; Spielberger & Rehiser, 2009). According to the Workplace Bullying Institute (2014), hierarchal bullying exists and thrives in the workplace because of fear:

> Fear of being the next target; fear of not helping correctly and botching it; fear of being the only one from a group to act; fear of retaliation by the bully; fear of loss of one's job and income. Thus, for coworkers

as well as targets themselves, the workplace becomes a fear-plagued environment. (para. 7)

Studies also showed if the employee complained to upper management or human resources, the employee was viewed as "anti-organizational" (Vickers, 2009, p. 262) and their claims were dismissed. Employees who complained about being bullied at work to upper management or those who attempted to file complaints against their managers were subjected to increased bullying efforts by their managers, which included "intimidation and threats of physical violence" (Vickers, 2009, p. 264). Because this is a power struggle from the top down, the employees with CTS are forced to do what their managers want them to do or risk reprimand and termination. The managers continue their bullying efforts until the employees submit (Roscigno et al., 2009b; Samnani, & Singh, 2012; Sloan et al., 2010; Vickers, 2009). In the employees' minds, the only way to get away from this type of persecution is to quit their job (Roscigno et al., 2009a; Sloan et al., 2010).

The effects of hierarchal bullying cause the bullied employee to experience a chain reaction of social, psychological, and psychosomatic symptoms and events in their professional and personal lives (Bartlett & Bartlett, 2011; Glasø, Nielsen, Einarsen, Haugland, & Mattheisen, 2009b; Hauge et al., 2010; Nixon et al., 2011;Tuckey, Dollard, Hosking, & Wienfield, 2009) that were found in numerous studies. Studies showed that employees who were bullied by their managers have a hard time socially trusting co-workers and colleagues in other positions (Bartlett & Bartlett, 2011; Glasø, Nielsen, & Einarsen, Haugland, & Mattheisen 2009b; Hauge et al., 2010; Tuckey et al., 2009) because the employer-employee work ethic was broken (Nixon et al., 2011; Roscigno et al., 2009b; Samnani & Singh, 2012). In the bullied employee's mind, work is supposed to provide opportunities for growth and advancement, not serve as the breeding ground for organized harassment, social injustice and inequities, and make you ill (Nixon et al., 2011).

The effects of being socially discredited and humiliation by their manager and co-workers causes the bullied employees to change their personality and forces them into isolation (Gholipour, Sanjari, Bod, & Kozekanan, 2011; Glasø et al., 2011). Numerous studies stated that because of the repeated abuse and humiliation endured socially for extended periods of time, bullied employees have high amounts of stress, anxiety, appear to be nervous all the time, and are insecure about their job (Nele, Flfi, & Hans, 2009; Gholipour, Sanjari, Bod, & Kozekanan, 2011; Vickers, 2009). Bullied employees were reported to have developed coping mechanisms such as grinding their teeth (Roscigno et al., 2009b; Vickers, 2009), nervous twitches (D'Cruz, & Noronha, 2010; Roscigno et al., 2009a; Vie et al., 2010) and developed dependency on "psychotropic drugs" (Niedhammer, Simone, Degioanni, Drummond, & Philip, 2010, p. 152).

In their personal lives, the continued and constant exposure to being bullied at work causes the employee to pull away from their spouse or partner both physically and sexually because they feared being rejected by them as well (Nielsen et al., 2012; O'Reilly & Aquino, 2011; Rugulies, 2012). In cases where extreme bullying occurred, bullied employees reported having thoughts of suicide because they felt this was the only way out of their oppression (Hinduja, 2009).

Research showed that the combination of psychological and psychosomatic effects of hierarchal bullying were traumatic to the bullied employee. Bullied employees reported developing depression, anxiety, (Murray, 2013; Nixon et al., 2011), irritability (Martin & Martin, 2010; McFarlane, 2013; Murray, 2013), and digestive disorders, such as Irritable Bowel Syndrome (Hogh, Hoel, & Carneiro, 2011; Martin & Martin, 2010). In extreme cases of hierarchal bullying, bullied employees developed Post Traumatic Stress Disorder (PTSD) and had to drop out of the work force because they were not able to distinguish their past experience of being bullied at work from their present job (McFarlane, 2013).

Lateral Bullying

Bullies pick their victims wisely. Bullies do not go after someone who can defend himself or herself or a strong willed person because the bullying tactics will not work on this type of individual (Glasø et al., 2011; McKay, Ciocirlan, & Chung, 2010). Instead, bullies target someone who is emotionally vulnerable and is unable to defend themselves because of their vulnerability (Gumbus & Meglich, 2012; McKay et al., 2010). Research shows that employers and co-workers often target employees with CTS because they are both physically and mentally vulnerable (Prime, Palmer, Kahn, & Goddard, 2010, Radat & Koleck, 2011; Richardson et al., 2009; Rugulies, 2012). Physically the employee with CTS is vulnerable because they are injured. Emotionally the employee with CTS is vulnerable because they were injured at work, while performing their everyday work duties. Research shows this tension is not only mentally but also emotionally draining (Idris et al., 2014; Schuhl & McMahon, 2006).

The employee with CTS is fighting an internal struggle to prove they can still do their job to their employer and themselves, along with knowing that if they continue to do their job, they risk re-aggravating their injury and possibly not being able to work at all (Pransky et al., 2002). The employee with CTS is also internally struggling with how they will pay their bills, feed their family, and meet their financial commitments such as paying their mortgage and keeping their home. From a bully's perspective, the employee with CTS is the perfect easy target because they are mentally and emotionally intertwined in their injury and will not be able to defend themselves from the bullies' attacks (Glasø et al., 2011; Kirsh et al., 2012).

Research also showed that work provides social structure, and there is a strong need to be socially accepted at work. Kirsh et al. (2012) and Kronstrom et al. (2011) argued that the importance of human interaction and social organizational acceptance in the workplace has a direct link on employees' mental and physical health. The social realm is where the bullies begin their attack. Research showed that bullies start their attacks by spreading rumors and gossiping about the employee with CTS (Carbo & Hughes, 2010). The bully centralizes the focus of their rumors and gossip about the employee by concentrating on the employees' weakness. This helps to establish credibility for the bullies' rumors and gossip and to discredit the employee at work (Brotheridge & Lee, 2010; Carbo & Hughes, 2010) by creating activating events. The activating events are meant to distract the employee with CTS from doing their job and focus their efforts on squashing the rumor. The bully now has proof positive that the employee with CTS is not doing their job effectively and is concentrating their efforts on other things. This evidence can be taken to the manager, and the employee with CTS is then questioned about their work habits and productivity. The second "activating event" (p. 729) has now occurred for the employee for now they have to prove they are performing at work in a professional manner.

The emotional impact of bullying on an employee with CTS has been shown to invoke negative responses towards their workplace

(Glaso et al., 2009a; Glaso et al., 2011). Anger, frustration, anxiety, and hopelessness are examples of negative responses (Glasø et al., 2009b), which when experienced over a long duration, "invoke feelings of irrevocable loss, and a sense of uncontrollability" (Vie et al., 2012, p. 166). The irrevocable loss the employee with CTS feels is loss of their work well-being (Spielberger & Reheiser, 2009). The employee remembers what it used to be like at work before they were injured and is saddened. Research shows when this occurs, the employee with CTS is now intertwined with their injury and must dodge the swirling affects that mentally seem to be all around them (Tracy et al., 2006).

The psychological effects of bullying have now taken their toll on the employee with CTS's mental and emotional health (Spielberger & Reheiser, 2009). The employee with CTS has been rendered inoperative and is confused and unable to understand what is happening (Glasø et al., 2009b; Spielberger & Reheiser, 2009). Because of this, the employees blame themselves for getting injured and for their injury (Pransky et al., 2012; Spielberger & Reheiser, 2009) as well as for their current state of well-being. Research showed that the employees' feelings of hopelessness about their injury and the inability to stop it from reoccurring have been shown to cause severe depression in employees with CTS (Glasø et al., 2009b; Spielberger & Reheiser, 2009). The bully continues this pattern until the employee is completely discredited in the eyes of their employer and the smallest of rumors and gossip sends the employee with CTS into panic attacks and "evolutionarily adaptive forms of action" (Vie et al., 2012, p. 167), such as the flee or fight response.

Financial Effects of Bullying

Workplace bullying proved to be a "key ethical problem in the modern workplace" (Boddy, 2011, p. 367) and had the opposite effect of what managers were trying to accomplish by bullying their employees into conforming (Montes et al., 2014). Studies showed that the social, psychological, and psychosomatic effects of employer bullying affected the organization's bottom line because of the waterfall of effects that bullied employees experience socially, psychologically, and psychosomatically (Agervold, 2009; Roscigno et al., 2009b). While minimal literature addressed the exact financial losses organizations experience due to bullying, literature implied that the losses to productivity (Atkinson, 2014; Vickers, 2009), employee turnover, excessive absenteeism, loss of product knowledge, and having to hire new personnel cost organizations between "6 to 36 billion" dollars (Stojanova, 2014, p. 149) annually.

Research also showed that bullied employees were not the only ones isolated and socially traumatized by workplace bullying (Ahlstrom et al., 2013; Dunstan & MacEachen, 2013). Studies showed bullying affects co-workers socially, psychologically, and psychosomatically as well. Employees left behind after their bullied co-worker left reported fear of who was going to be the next bullied target or victim, decreased morale (Beirne & Hunter, 2012; MacIntosh, 2012), increased job insecurity, psychological and physical stress levels (Davidson & Harrington, 2012; Gumbus & Meglich, 2012; Law et al., 2011; MacIntosh, 2012), "job burnout" (Georgakopoulos, Wilkin, & Kent, 2011, p. 5), and eventually they began to experience and exhibit some of the same symptoms and ailments that their bullied co-worker did (Idris et al., 2014). Researchers stated this progression was caused by a combination of viewing their co-worker under stress and the guilt the co-workers felt for not helping the bullied employee (Dunstan & MacEachen, 2013; Idris et al., 2014).

Employer bullying also jeopardized the reputation of the organization (Armstrong, 2011; Gumbus & Lyons, 2011; Hollins Martin & Martin, 2010; MacIntosh, 2012; Wiedmer, 2011) because of numerous lawsuits filed by bullied employees. While research showed that three-fourths of the lawsuits filed against employers for bullying were ruled in favor of the employer, the social effects of the law suit itself caused doubts about the organization with their clients (Appelbaum et al., 2012; Gumbus & Meglich, 2012).

While research leant heavily in favor of enacting an anti-bullying law, it can be argued that bad management is everywhere and some are worse than others. Additionally, it can be argued if the employees are truly miserable at work or feel they are being treated unfairly, they do have the right to seek employment elsewhere. In instances where the employee is socially, psychologically, and psychosomatically damaged, counseling and therapy is recommended to help undo the sociological, psychological, and psychosomatic damage that was done before the employee starts a new job in order to help alleviate the symptoms and put the experience in the past.

Additional research is recommended to learn how much employer bullying does physically cost an organization annually. Research findings can then be used and presented to upper management as an argument for instituting anti-bullying programs within the organization. Because of the devastating effects bullying has caused in the workplace, further research is recommended which would examine the influence other areas of the organization can have on preventing bullying.

Employees' Perspectives

Research has shown there is a strong need to be socially accepted at work, because work provides social structure. Therefore, it can be argued that workplace well-being is no longer limited to an employee's being content to having a job. Rather, in today's society, employment is viewed as "the key to social membership" (Fevre et al., 2013, p. 288). However, research has also shown that the key to social membership is very fragile, and when its social base is disrupted or threatened, the same key that was once used to unlock societal acceptance is now being used to lock out those deemed socially unacceptable. Kirsh et al. (2012) and Kronstrom et al. (2011) argued the importance of human interaction and social organizational acceptance in the workplace has a direct link on employees' mental and physical health. Research has shown that the result of being shunned in the workplace by formerly accepting employers and co-workers has overwhelming psychological and psychosomatic effects to the employee with CTS (Houshmand et al., 2012; Miner-Rubino & Reed, 2010; Skakon, Nielsen, Borg, & Guzman, 2010).

Kirsh et al. (2012) argued when social acceptance is forcibly taken away, employees with CTS experience "a loss of identity" (p. 147) and begin to identify themselves with their disease (Lavie-Ajayi, Almog, & Krumer-Nevo, 2012). Lavie-Ajayi et al. argued when employees with CTS begins to identify themselves with their disease, rather than their position, they take on a whole new classification in their minds, and they socially start to shut down. When this occurs, the psychological and psychosomatic battle of CTS begins for the employees. Research has shown that it takes a very strong willed and determined person to overcome being socially shunned and battle psychological and psychosomatic effects all at once (Ramirez-Maestre, Esteve, & Lopez, 2012). To adequately demonstrate the effects of these consequences this section of the literature review will discuss the professional and personal sociological, psychological, and psychosomatic effects of CTS and how they directly contribute to employee's over-all physical well-being.

Professional Psychological Disease Effects of CTS

In the multiple studies concerning CTS and its effects, one of the re-occurring themes present for employees with CTS was the total impact of this disease. Studies showed employees with CTS have numerous fears about the affect CTS will have on their professional lives, which include fear of job loss, rate of job satisfaction (Jerosch, Shepstone, Wilson, Dyer, & Blake, 2014; Thomsen, Björk, & Cederlund, 2014), poor job performance (Atroshi, Lyren, & Gummesson, 2009; Hammond & Harris, 2012), their injury returning (Roll, 2011), and future employment opportunities (Wyatt, Jones, & Veale, 2013). Literature revealed that CTS has a direct link to sociological, psychological, and psychosomatic problems. Research also showed that the fears employees have about the effects of CTS do not compare to the onset of psychological and psychosomatic effects and consequences that will plague them if they are left to fester (Ramirez-Maestre et al., 2012; Radat & Koleck, 2011; Schumann et al., 2014).

Research showed that in addition to work's providing social acceptance (Fevre et al., 2013), it is also how people self-identify and form their self-identity (Lavie-Ajayi et al., 2013). Lavie-Ajayi et al. (2013) argued that people identify themselves with the job or position they hold. It is one of the first questions people ask when they meet someone, *What do you do for a living?* The response is *I am a....* When there is no job or position to identify, the open-ended internal question for employees with CTS becomes, *Who am I?* Research showed if this question goes unanswered, the employee with CTS begins to relate who they are to their disease, rather than their career (Lavie-Ajayi et al., 2013).

Ramirez-Maestre et al. (2012) argued when this occurs, the employee with CTS has socially shut down and accepted their fate based on the effects their disease will have on them (Heijbel et al., 2006; Niedhammer et al., 2010; O'Reilly & Aquino, 2011). This includes job loss, lack of job satisfaction, and not being able to perform at their job as they once did (Heijbel et al., 2006). Niedhammer et al. (2010) argued it is the acceptance of their fate that psychologically paralyzes the employee with CTS and keeps them from moving forward and helping themselves: "Too paralyzed to move forward, and not wanting to remember life before being inflicted with their disease" (p. 157). The employees with CTS psychologically give up on themselves.

When this occurs, Niedhammer et al. (2010) stated, the psychosomatic effects of CTS chip away at the employee with CTS's well-being. Studies showed employees with CTS have more reported sick days than employees with other injuries (Hinduja, 2009; Hogh et al., 2011; Nixon et al., 2011); developed depression, anxiety, and sleep disorders (Idris et al., 2014; Mug Kang et al., 2011); have low self-esteem (Idris et al., 2014); developed digestive disorders (Idris et al., 2014; Kirsh et al., 2012), and hypertension.

Professional and Personal Life Struggles

Professional. Studies revealed that employees utilized different coping strategies for dealing with their own professional and personal psychological fears about CTS. In their professional life, research showed that the mental and emotional shock of having contracted CTS caused employees to feel helpless against their injury. Studies showed that fear is what keeps employees with CTS for asking for help from their employers. In Hoefsmit et al.'s (2013) study, one employ with CTS said, "You have to learn to read between what your boss is saying and what they actually mean. They tell you they want to help you, but they are really looking for a way to get rid of you. The better you are interpreting, the longer you stay employed" (Hoefsmit et al., 2013, p. 156).

Hoefsmit et al. (2013) argued that this is a psychological play on words on the employer's part. Studies showed that when an employer is not honest with the employee with CTS, this further intensifies the situation because the employee with CTS is already dealing with the sociological, psychological, and psychosomatic effects of CTS. Adding to the mental and emotional stress of the worries and fears employees with CTS have about losing their jobs only makes matters worse and makes the employee with CTS feel psychologically abused by their employer (Hinduja, 2009; Hoefsmit et al., 2013). Additional studies showed that having to read into the true meaning of what their employer is saying caused them to be suspicious of everything and everyone around them (Gumbus & Lyons, 2011; Hinduja, 2009; Murray, 2013; Niedhammer et al., 2010).

Studies also showed when the employee with CTS figures out their employer is intentionally trying to remove them from the workplace, it is already too late (Hauge et al., 2010; Idris et al., 2014). This has been shown to cause extreme cases of anxiety, depression, and panic attacks for the employee with CTS. The employees feel helpless to do anything, because in their minds, their injury is what caused this situation to occur. Employees reported feeling physically engulfed by the effects of their stress (Murray, 2013; Niedhammer et al., 2010). One employee stated, "It felt like was swirling all around me and there was nothing I could do to stop it" (Niedhammer et al., 2010, p. 157). Other employees with CTS stated that "they feel trapped" (Idris et al., 2014, p. 298) and "stuck in the middle of a bad dream" (p. 299) which is playing out right before their eyes. Because of the psychological effects of this disease, employees with CTS feel mentally and physically drained (Idris et al., 2014; Koukoulaiki, 2013; Niedhammer et al., 2010).

Despite its sociological, psychological, and psychosomatic effects, research showed that employees with CTS want to work and stay employed (Persson et al., 2014; Riach & Loretto, 2009). However, when it hurts to work, work becomes a struggle and another activating event for the employee with CTS. In one study, an employee with CTS stated, "It's hard to type when your wrist is throbbing or three out of five of your fingers go numb" (Opsteegh et al., 2009, p. 248). Employees with CTS are very self-conscious about their injuries, and when they have to wear a brace and answer repeated questions about their injuries, they become even more aware that they are not like their co-workers no matter how hard they try to be.

Numerous studies made the argument that employees with CTS just want to blend in like everyone else at work (Opsteegh et al., 2009; O'Rourke, 2014; Palazzo, Ravaud, Papelard, Ravaud, & Poiraudeau, 2014; Parenteau et al., 2011), but as one employee with CTS stated, "It's hard when comments are made to you about your brace. You become very self-conscious" (Opsteegh et al., 2009, p. 248). Employees with CTS also hide their symptoms and coping mechanisms while they are at work. Researchers argued that employees with CTS do this because they feel different from their co-workers, and drawing further attention to their differences and their injuries "makes it that much easier to get rid of them" (Parenteau et al., 2011, p. 418).

After experiencing the physical effects of CTS, Koh, Moate, and Grinsell (2009) argued the psychological effects of the disease emerge because the employee is afraid to return to work, afraid of their injury returning, and afraid of their careers ending. Marras, Cutlip, Burt, and Waters (2009) argued that employees who are inflicted with carpal tunnel syndrome are fighting a psychological struggle within themselves, because while they need to work, the employee with CTS also know that their job is what made them ill. McFarlane (2013) argued the psychological struggle for the employee with CTS comes full circle when the employee accepts the reality that if they continue to perform the same duties at their job, their injury will most likely return. Self-identity in the workplace was also noted as part of the psychological struggle employees with CTS encounter because in addition to work's providing social acceptance (Fevre et al., 2013), it also provides structure as people identify themselves with their professions (O'Rourke, 2014; Silva, Sampaio, Mancini, Luz, & Alcantara, 2010).

Bartlett and Bartlett (2011) argued that it is the psychological struggle of this disease that forces the employee into "counterproductive workplace behaviors" (Bartlett, & Bartlett, 2011, p. 69) because instead of the employee doing their job, the employee with CTS attempts to prove to themselves and their organization that they are still capable of functioning in the workplace. Research showed this added undue stress to the employee with CTS because now they feel they have to prove their self-worth in the organization and show that they are still capable of doing their job in the same manner as before they were injured (Brouwer et al., 2009; Côté & Coutu, 2010). W. Kong et al. (2012), Board & Brown (2010), and King, Tang, Yu, Luo, Liang, and He (2011) strongly recommend psychological treatment along with rehabilitation to help ease the injured employee's fears about returning to work and how they will be treated by their co-workers and management. Marras et al. concurred and argued the significance and impact that "psychosocial and organizational factors have on each other, is "multidimensional" (p. 15).

Westgaard and Winkel (2010) argued "resonant management style, information, support, group autonomy and procedural justice were modifiers with favorable influence on outcome" (p. 261). However, employees with CTS reported additional stress-induced physical symptoms brought on by their managers' "one size fits all approach" (Egan et al., 2009, p. 8) to their illness. Nixon et al. (2011) confirmed the link between stress and the effects it had on employees with CTS additional symptoms. According to Nixon et al. (2011), "when an employee encounters an event that their body evaluates as harmful or threatening" (p. 2), their body reacts in one of three ways: "alarm, exhaustion, flight-or-fight" (p. 3). Additional studies showed that employees with CTS who felt they had no support network at work succumbed to "psychological strain" (Clay & Olitt, 2012), took longer to heal within the RTW (Clay & Olitt, 2012; Hepburn et al., 2010), succumbed to depression (Druss, Hwang, Petukhova, Sampson, & Kessler, 2009; Franche et al., 2007; Hepburn et al., 2010), and "wanted to quit" (Wright, 2009, p. 15) their jobs. Kosny et al. (2013) argued that employees who felt they had to prove their injuries' legitimacy to their co-workers felt isolated, alone, and disillusioned with their legitimacy and the legitimacy of the organization as a whole (De Cuyper et al., 2009; Dunstan & MacEachen, 2013; Kosny et al., 2013). However, those who had the support of their manager and co-workers displayed "psychological well-being" (Gilbreath, 2012, p. 790) at work, which included "self-efficacy, mental and emotional competencies, organizational-based self-esteem, and optimism" (p. 791).

Personal. Anger, frustration, depression, loss of self-identity, and having to prove self-worth (Dow, Roche, & Ziebland, 2012; Radat & Koleck, 2011; Vroman, Warner, & Chamberlain, 2009) were shown in research as part of the psychological struggles and bias employees with CTS encountered in their personal lives. Because work provides social acceptance (Fevre et al., 2013), it also provides social structure and balance (DeSouza, & Frank, 2011) because people identify themselves in their personal lives with their professions (O'Rourke, 2014; Silva et al., 2010). Research showed when this identity is taken away, employees with CTS trade their professional identity for their illness as an identity in a process known as *narratological distress*:

> Narratological distress is the internal battle between two unwanted narratives: The elusive delegitimizing narrative of denial, which seeks to ignore the experience of pain; and the narrative that acknowledges the pain, but with the price of accepting oneself as "ill" or "disabled." (Lavie-Ajayi et al., 2013, p. 192)

Once this occurs, the downward psychological spiral begins, and employees with CTS concentrate their efforts on blaming others for their injury rather than trying to cope and deal with their injury (Banerjee,

Bhattacharya, & Sanyal, 2014; Cano et al., 2009; Ramirez-Maestre et al., 2012). Studies showed this condition placed significant stress on other family members and personal relationships because family members had to take on the roles and responsibility for the employee with CTS (Tsao, 2012; West, Usher, Foster, & Stewart, 2012). Negative thoughts were also prevalent in the research because the employees with CTS felt they had lost everything and blamed their employers and those around them for their disease (Cano et al., 2009; Cho et al., 2012; Richardson et al., 2009).

Research also revealed the opposite happened when the employee had a strong support network at home. In instances where the family members were supportive of the employee with CTS, the employee learned how to come to grips with their disease (Gauthier, Thibault, & Sullivan, 2011; Parenteau et al., 2011; Pulvers & Hood, 2013) and found ways to overcome its effects in their personal lives (West, Usher, Foster, & Stewart, 2011).

Economic hardship was the other factor cited in studies. In the United States in 1995 according to Prime et al. (2010), "400, 000 to 500, 000" (p. 354) employees with CTS underwent surgical nerve decompression surgery to relieve their symptoms and missed an average of "27 days" (Lewis, Mauffrey, Newman, Lambert, & Hull, 2009, p. 445) of work per year. According to Lewis et al. (2009), this equated to "over 2.8 billion" (p. 445) dollars in lost wages for employees with CTS. By 2012, the Nonfatal Occupational Injuries and Illnesses Requiring Days Away from Work report was released by the United States Department of Labor Statistics, which stated "Musculoskeletal disorders, (MSDs), commonly known as ergonomic injuries, accounted for 34 percent of all workplace injuries" (U.S. Bureau of Labor Statistics, 2013, para. 52), and "there were 388,060 MSDs, with an incident rate of 38 cases per 10,000 full-time workers" (para. 53).

Additional economic hardships that were cited in various studies included having to change jobs and accept a lower base salary (Palazzo et al., 2014; Welch, Haile, Boden, & Hunting, 2010), "unemployment" (Organization for Economic Cooperation and Development, 2009, p. 1), waiting an extensively long period for Workers Compensation payments to be received (Abasolo, Lajas, Leon, Carmona, & Macarron, 2012; W. Young, 2009), and having to pay out of pocket cost for medications and treatments. O'Conner (2009) stated that the estimated prescription cost for suffers of carpal tunnel syndrome ranged close to a thousand dollars a year.

No literature discussed how employees with CTS met their financial commitments, the steps or measures they took in order to try and met their financial commitments, or the end result of their not being able to meet their financial commitments. Additional research is recommended to uncover the answers to these questions and how they personally affect the employee with CTS's psychological well-being. Additionally, when the employee is socially, psychologically, and psychosomatically damaged, counseling and therapy is recommended to help undo the sociological, psychological, and psychosomatic damage that was done before the employee starts a new job in order to help alleviate the symptoms and put the past in the past.

Chapter 3

Methodology

The purpose of this grounded theory study was to discover how the physical, social, and emotional effects of carpal tunnel syndrome (CTS) affect employees with CTS's ability to complete an employer-sponsored return to work (RTW) program at their place of employment. Using a constructivist approach, relationships between employees, their managers, and their co-workers will be examined. Personal needs in this study will be demonstrated through the employees' morals, values, and ethics as they relate to CTS and how the employee with CTS performs, or does not perform in their employer-sponsored RTW program. The results found in these relationships were compared to the business needs, healthcare needs, and personal needs showing how they compared, contrasted, and coexisted with each other. Participants in this study consisted of 12 employees with CTS in three separate companies who were participating in their employers' RTW programs. The purpose behind using three separate companies was to show the differences and similarities within the study between participants and employers as they relate to CTS.

The guiding questions for this study were:

RQ1. How does an employee afflicted with carpal tunnel syndrome's morals, values, and ethics dictate his or her success or failure rate for completing a RTW program?

RQ2. How much impact does an injured employee's psychological makeup have on how well he or she will perform at his or her job after returning from a workplace injury?

RQ3. How do the effects of employer's bias towards employees with CTS affect the employee's successful completion rate of a RTW program?

RQ4. How does an employer's morals, values, and ethics dictate whether he or she will implement a RTW program for employees inflicted with CTS?

RQ5. How do co-workers psychologically affect an employee with CTS's completion rate in an employer-sponsored RTW program?

Constructivist Grounded theory provided the methodological framework for investigating the research questions because of the individuality brought to the study through each of the participants' morals, values, and ethics. When seen through an interpretivist lens, the participants' individuality helps to reveal the essence of societal influence towards the shaping of a RTW program for employees with CTS. By using this method, the researcher can contrive theories by "learning about the experience within embedded, hidden networks, situations and relationships" (Creswell, 2009, p. 65). This approach was consistent with the central phenomenon being studied because the goal was to measure the determinants of why an employee does or does not complete the employer-sponsored RTW program.

Research Design

Qualitative Research Design

Unlike quantitative research, qualitative research is difficult to define, because it does not subscribe to a set of theories or paradigms that are relatively, distinctively its own. Qualitative research does not lead participants in a study through a subscribed set of questions that are used on each participant in the study and then utilized to generate statistical data, generalize meaning, and generate a theory. Rather, qualitative research emerges the researcher into a social setting in an attempt to reveal its idiosyncrasies and complexities, so the researcher can learn the who, what, when, where, why and to what extent the elements physically, psychologically, psychometrically, psychosomatically, and sociologically each exist within each other, why they exist this way, and why they are socially accepted to exist this way. Ritchie, Lewis, McNaughton Nicholls, and Ormston (2013) argued, "qualitative research is a situated activity that locates the observer in the world. It consists of a set of interpretive, material practices that makes the world visible" (p. 3).

In its attempt to make the world visible, qualitative research deals with people, their morals, values, and ethics, which in turn shape and mold their idiosyncrasies, their fears, their hopes, their dreams, their wants and desires individually. This adds even more complexity to an already complex topic, people, because it can be argued that no two people are exactly alike in every aspect. Therefore, because no two people are alike, their morals, values, and ethics are as individual as they are.

According to Crewsell (2009), the premise behind qualitative research is to uncover a deep understanding of the subjective experiences of the participants in the study. This is accomplished through uncovering the participants' feelings and emotions as they relate to a specific event or social setting. Creswell (2009) and Strauss and Corbin (1998) argued that qualitative research allows insight into the material being studied because data is gathered directly from the participants' words, feelings, and experiences as they tell their story about a particular social experience. Patton (2002) and Maxwell (2012) argued that the participants' experience is what gives value to qualitative research because the human experience is unique, individual, and personal and therefore cannot be categorized; reliance on preset molds, menus, one–size-fits-all approaches, or "linear models" are untenable in qualitative research (Maxwell, 2012, p. 85). Rather, the participants' stories, feelings, emotions, facial expressions, and body language drive the data, the study's direction, re-direction, and eventually lead the researchers to their conclusions. Patton (2002) argued that qualitative research is holistic in its awareness of the human phenomenon because "the whole is greater than the sum of its parts and, therefore, describes a way of looking at an issue that is all-inclusive, systematic, and that cannot be reduced to its component parts (p. 84). Creswell (2009) further argued that qualitative research supports "a way of looking at research that honors an inductive style, a focus on individual, and the importance of rendering the complexity of a situation" (p. 4).

Patton (2002) and Maxwell (2012) argued that the value of qualitative research lies in the fact that not all questions can be answered with numbers or statistics or have numerical or statistical value directly placed on them. Rather, in qualitative research, data is collected though observations, body language, semi-structured interviews, and open-ended questions that enable the participant in a qualitative study to open up and share their experience surrounding the phenomenon being studied, rather than relying on casual models or theories to draw its conclusions (Creswell, 2009; Patton, 2002). Though the participants' own words, actions, and reactions, the human experience regarding a specific social situation unfolds and is revealed. Maxwell (2012) argued that the human experience cannot be measured by "a choice from a prior menu or a linear model, because in qualitative research, there isn't an unvarying order in which the different tasks or components must be arranged, nor a linear relationship among the components of a design" (p. 2).

Maxwell further argued that in order to "design a qualitative study, you can't just develop (or borrow) a logical strategy in advance and then implement it faithfully" (p. 3), because qualitative research requires the researcher to assess and reassess how the design and process is working and adjust and readjust based upon the direction the research has taken. When the research is complete, it is up to the researcher to draw conclusions based upon participants' experiences, rather than forcing it to fit a specific mold, variance, or specific methodology (Maxwell, 2012). This is what separates qualitative data from quantitative data; "rather than testing theory" (Merriam, 2009, p. 6), qualitative data "inductively analyzes a social phenomenon" (p. 6). Through qualitative research, the impacts and effects of social, psychological, and emotional crucibles are depicted.

Qualitative research does not seek to define social existence. Rather, qualitative research shows how individual social identities exist though the thoughts, feelings, and stories of the participants' social, psychological, and psychosomatic experiences. Though the participants' thoughts, feelings, emotions, and fears, an individual story emerges. Research has shown when multiple individual stories emerge and centralize around one or more ideas, a pattern emerges that can take the researcher to the depths of the participants' most inner thoughts, feelings, fears, and motivations to investigate why they responded or reacted a particular way, in a particular situation, on a particular day (Maxwell, 2012; Merriam, 2009; Ritchie et al., 2013).

Qualitative research seeks to understand how the physical, psychological, psychosomatic, and sociological experiences people have in the world as they come in contact with each other have the ability and influence to produce the cause and effect reactions that eventually lead to the production of physical, psychological, psychosomatic, and sociological effects in individuals. In order to do this, researchers must submerse themselves into the root of the issue "in order to understand the plethora of unlimited social boundaries and acceptance that exist in society as a norm today" (Patton, 2002, p. 40). Additionally, researchers should not lock themselves into preconceived notions or theories of what they feel the study should uncover or reveal (Patton, 2002) because qualitative research designs cannot be manipulated or controlled in order to produce a particular set of results. Rather, researchers have to be open and willing to follow the data wherever it may lead them and "adapt the nature of the questions in order to pursue deep and holistic understanding of the psychological and sociological issues surrounding the phenomenon" (Corbin & Strauss, 2008, p. 15). This mindset is essential and crucial when conducting qualitative research because it allows researchers to echo the participants' essence of their experience through "open-ended, non-manipulative, and non-controlling nature of naturalistic inquiry" (Corbin & Strauss, 2008, p. 19).

Study Methodology

A grounded theory methodology that specifically uses a constructivist grounded approach is appropriate for the type of data I will be collecting, because people use their experiences to define and relate to their reality, and "constructivism is a research paradigm that denies the existence of an objective reality" (Guba & Lincoln, 1989, p. 43). Constructivism "asserts that realities are social constructions of the mind, and that there exist as many such constructions as there are individuals" (Guba & Lincoln, 1989, p. 43). Charmaz (2014) argued that data does not provide a window on reality. Rather, reality is discovered from the "interactive process and its temporal, cultural, and structural contexts" (p. 524).

Therefore, in the case of this study, bringing individualized morals, values and ethics into the examination of the RTWs will reveal the impact societal influence has in the workplace. Through the use of an interpretivist lens, "mere statements of uniformities of social behavior in responses to social influences" (Guba & Lincoln, 1989, p. 12) can be captured and depicted and used to illustrate the direct influence on the outcome for an employee with CTS in an RTW. This view is consistent with the central phenomenon in this study because I am trying to measure the determinants of why an employee does or does not complete the employer-sponsored RTW program. In order to do this and satisfy the research question, the words of those undergoing the experience must remain intact. In order to do this, I must construct theory as an outcome of their interpretation of the participants' "stories, which depict how the participants construct their worlds" (Guba & Lincoln, 1989, p. 85).

In this study, the inner workings and effects that workplace relationships have on employees with CTS will be examined through the morals, values, and ethics of the employees with CTS. Because the workplace is made up of "multiple individual realities influenced by context" (Mills et al., 2006, p. 7), these relationships have to be explored to understand why employees with CTS think, feel, and react the way they do in an employer-sponsored RTW.

Current studies dealing with CTS measure either the physical aspect of the disease through case studies or its psychological impacts through phenomenological studies. However, case studies and phenomenological studies fail to show how the physical limitations of CTS impact its psychological effects and how the psychological effects of CTS impact the employees' physical performance in the workplace. The conceptual theoretical framework for this study focused on the "interrelationships" (Miles & Huberman, 1994, p. 19) between the employee with CTS, their co-workers, and their managers. A conceptual diagram showed how the injured employees' fears can affect their behavior at work. Focusing on the effects that interrelationships have in the workplace formed a connection between the psychological and physical effects of CTS. By focusing on the effects that interrelationships have in the workplace, the research gap was filled because at the end of the study, an overall, encompassing picture of the disease, which included its effects and the human experience in the workplace, was revealed.

The use of constant comparison, "memoing and diagramming" (Mills et al., 2006, p. 3), results in the emergence of patterns that establish and reveal "meanings about values, beliefs, and ideologies" (p. 7) as they relate to employees with CTS. These patterns, once established and coded, illuminate the overall impact of CTS in the workplace. Employers can use this information to develop individualized RTW programs to address all of the issues and help their employees fully heal and return to work.

Sample

The population for this study consisted of 12 people in three separate companies who have been afflicted with CTS and were absent from work for an extended period of time in order for their injury to heal. Participants in this study were either returning to work after their extended absence or had returned to work within the last 45 days and were actively participating in their employer's RTW program. In order for employees with CTS to participate in this study, they had to provide proof of a previous licensed physician's diagnosis of CTS.

At the start of the study, theoretical sampling required finding employees with CTS who were participating in their employers' RTW programs. I placed recruitment material at local physical rehabilitation centers, hospitals, doctor offices, chiropractic offices, alternative medicine offices, grocery stores, and on social media pages that were specific to carpal tunnel syndrome. Potential participants who indicated interest received information regarding the study, which consisted of the IRB-approved study recruitment poster and the informational recruitment Power Point presentation. Participants who wished to participate in the study clicked on an e-mail link to contact the researcher and state that they wished to participate in the study.

Quota sampling was used to recruit participants up to the age of 55. The age limit was imposed because by age 55, people are close to retirement and research showed that by age 55 some employees who regularly used computers were experiencing additional hand medical symptoms, such as arthritis (Munnell, 2015). According to the Center for Retirement Research (as cited in Munnell, 2015), men retire approximately at age 65 and women at age 62. Quota sampling continued at initial on-site interviews at a location specified by the participants or in Skype interviews for more remotely located participants. During the initial on-site interviews, participants shared specifics about their injuries. Participants who could not provide specific information about their injuries were excluded from the study.

Additionally, employees who did not meet the specified inclusion criteria were excluded from the study. The inclusion criteria for this study were (a) previous diagnosis of CTS by a licensed physician; (b) the employee's CTS had to be work related; (c) the employee with CTS had to accept Workers Compensation benefits for their CTS; (d) the employee with CTS had to receive some form of treatment for their CTS that required them to be off of work longer than 30 days; (e) the employee with CTS had to be willing to participate in their employer's RTW program; (f) participants could be either male or female; (g) employees with CTS had to be under the age of 55; (h) employees with CTS had to be willing to be interviewed and have their interviews audio recorded; (i) employees with CTS had to be willing to sign a waiver, which stated they were prohibited from directly discussing the study and its findings with other employees, managers, or human resource personnel; and (j) the employee with CTS had to be able to recall specific information about their injury at the time of the initial on-site interview.

The exclusion criteria for this study were (a) the employee with CTS diagnosed him- or herself with CTS; (b) the employee with CTS was not following their doctor's treatment programs; (c) the employee with CTS was not willing to participate in their employer's RTW program; (d) the employee with CTS was not willing to be interviewed and have the interview audio taped; (e) the employee with CTS did not accept Workers Compensation benefits; (f) the employee with CTS planned on suing their employer for their injury; (f) the employee with CTS was over the age of 55; (g) the employee with CTS was not off of work for a minimum of 30 days; (h) the employees' CTS was not work related; (i) the employee with CTS was not willing to sign the waiver, which prohibited them from discussing the study and its findings with other employees, managers, or human resource personnel; and (j) the employee with CTS could not answer specific questions about their injury at the time of the initial on-site interview.

Participants were selected based on their meeting the inclusion criteria and being able to provide specific information about their injury at the time of the initial on-site interviews. Theoretical sampling was consistent with constructivist grounded theory because it required the participants in this study to be able to recall specifics about their injuries, the treatment they received within their employers' RTW programs, and how their co-workers treated them after they returned to work. Though the participants' thoughts, feelings, emotions, and fears, their individual stories emerged and provided insight into social existence in the workplace for people with CTS. The use of the employee with CTS's words and experiences allowed specifics about the physical, psychological, psychosomatic, and sociological experiences to be used to construct theories, which showed how the cause and effect reactions are the motivating factors of why an employee with CTS acted or reacted a particular way, in a particular situation on a particular day (Maxwell, 2012; Merriam, 2009; Ritchie et al., 2013). Five men and seven women participated in this study.

Setting

Participants in this study had the option to pick the location where the on-site, semi-structured interviews would be conducted. Six interviews took place at the public library in the conference room. To ensure the participants' privacy at the library and also to help them feel comfortable discussing their injury, because CTS is a personal experience (DiCicco-Bloom & Crabtree, 2006), I reserved the conference room under a pseudonym, and I changed the pseudonym for each interview. Additionally, I made arrangements with the library staff to gain permission to hang a sign on the door, which said Do Not Disturb. The door was also locked and the curtains were drawn. Chairs were arranged so the participants and the researcher faced each other. The audio recording device sat between the researcher and participants on the table during the interview to ensure that all questions and responses were clearly heard.

At the start of every semi-structured interview, I stated my name, the date and time the interview was taking place, and the participant's computer generated number. Participants confirmed their computer-generated number, along with their signature on the consent form. At the start of the semi-structured interviews, participants received a copy of the semi-structured questions that would be asked during the interview. Participants could answer the questions in any order, but they must respond to every question. I informed participants that I would not lead the interview; instead, I was there to learn about their experience. The semi-structured interviews lasted between 60 and 90 minutes and varied depending upon the participants' recollection of the experience they were describing.

I took notes during the semi-structured interview in a notebook that was designated for the specified participant. To ensure the participants' privacy and anonymity, the notebook was color-specific to the participants' computer generated numbers. I kept this coded information on a password-protected portable jump drive and brought only the notebook that was specific to the participant being interviewed to the on-site semi-structured interview. When multiple semi-structured interviews were going to take place during the day, I kept the color-specific notebooks locked in the trunk of my vehicle. Additionally, if multiple semi-structured interviews were going to take place at the same location, I scheduled them far enough apart to ensure that the participants would not accidentally see each other and that I allowed enough time to change color-specific notebooks. At the end of every semi-structured interview, the researcher collected the copy of the interview questions from the participant and reminded the participant that they agreed at the initial interview that they would not discuss the semi-structured questions or the study with anyone. After the participant acknowledged this statement and verbally agreed not to discuss the semi-structured interview and the study, the recording device was turned off and I waited until the participant left the room before turning the recording device back on and recording specifics about the interview.

Some interviews took place in other locations, one in the conference room in the village hall that was located near the participant's home and two in the basement of the participants' church. All interviews employed the same protocol that was used in the library setting. Three interviews took place via Skype because two of the participants were located out of state, and one participant did not live within commuting distance. In these instances, I conducted the interviews in my home office, with the door shut and the curtains drawn in order to ensure the participants' privacy. I turned the camera to show the participants this private setting before every interview.

Instrumentation/Measures

Instruments

Data collection instruments for this study were (a) semi-structured interviews, (b) observations, (c) open-ended questions, (d) and the researcher. Semi-structured interviews served as the foundation for the creation of open-ended questions. The purpose of the semi-structured interviews was to learn about the initial background of the participants' experience with CTS in the workplace. Observations, in conjunction with the semi-structured interviews, confirmed or supplemented the participants' responses. Observations also suggested open-ended interview questions.

Open-ended questions used for the interviews allowed participants to open up about their experience of how they dealt with having CTS in the workplace, how they were treated in and out of the RTW program, and why they feel they were treated the way they were. Direct questions were only used for clarification purposes. The open-ended questions utilized a conversational style and were intended to make the participant comfortable and at ease discussing their feelings about their injuries and how they felt they were treated at work and within the RTW program.

Semi-structured interviews, observations, and open-ended research questions gave participants the ability to open up about their experiences. This in turn addressed the research questions and illuminated how the effects of the psychological, psychosomatic, and sociological served as the exposition of why a participant acted and reacted the way he or she did within the RTW. This data, collected and compiled in the interview transcripts and observations, allowed the generation of a theory (Strauss & Corbin, 1998).

The semi-structured questions used in this study follow. In order to accommodate the 60 to 90 minute time frame, the questions were broken apart in order to allow participants significant time per semi-structured interview segment to adequately discuss each one.

1. Describe the scenario of how you first realized there was something wrong with your wrist.
2. Can you describe what you do for a living that caused you to contract carpal tunnel syndrome?
3. How or why did you go into this line of work?
4. What does carpal tunnel syndrome mean to you?
5. What about your job would you change in order to continue doing it?
6. What is your greatest fear about your injury?
7. Why are you afraid of your injury?
8. Can you tell me about a time when someone said a word or phrase and you had a negative reaction to it?

9. Describe the carpal tunnel syndrome pain you are feeling at this moment.

10. When you stretch and take your medication, do you do so publicly or do you do it in private? Please explain why.

11. Can you tell me what personal modifications you have made for yourself at work in order to continue to do your job and minimize your carpal tunnel syndrome symptoms?

12. What are some of the comments that your co-workers made to you today that you feel were in direct correlation with your injury?

13. How has your relationship between you and your co-workers changed in the last three months?

14. What physical, emotional, and social factors make you uncomfortable being at work?

15. How do you think your employers and co-workers view your injury?

16. What factors related to your injury make you think you are in jeopardy of losing your job?

17. How do you relate your mental well-being towards your injury?

18. What was your work situation like before you got injured? Explain in detail.

19. What factors related to your injury make you feel that your work situation has changed because you got injured?

20. Can you tell me what you do at work to minimize the pain from your injury so your co-workers and manager do not know how much physical pain you are in?

21. How do you see yourself today in terms of your injury and being able to physically and mentally able to function in your job?

22. Many doctors recommend immobilizing a wrist in a brace while performing work activities. How has wearing a brace impacted your life at work with your co-workers and managers?

23. How do you perceive your ability to do your job now that you are injured?

24. Can you tell me about a time when you felt you identified more with your job than your injury?

25. Can you tell me about a time when you felt you identified more with your injury than your job?

Researcher as an Instrument

I was responsible for all facets of this study which included (a) recruiting participants, (b) conducting study qualification, (c) collecting and collating individual participant data, (d) securing interview sites, (e) analyzing and interpreting data, and (f) final write up. Patton (2002) made the argument that credible qualitative research comes from "the methodology in terms of fieldwork, the strength of the researcher, and the belief of the researcher in the value of the qualitative research" (p. 45). My combined 15 years of business experience, five years of educational experience, and prior scholarly research accomplished this credibility.

I understood the necessity for confidentiality and how to ensure it. In the business world, I served as a project manager and business analyst in the healthcare industry and the Republican Party. While working in the healthcare industry, I was exposed to individual personal and private information, which included individual healthcare records, employment records, household information, including previous and current addresses, income, banking information, and social security numbers. Identify theft and HIPAA fines would have been the result had this personal information been leaked (Letzring & Snow, 2011; Seitz, 2010).

Additionally, while working in the Republican Party during a recall election, I had to ensure and maintain absolute anonymity and maintain the candidates' confidentiality. I heard political conversations, political strategies, political campaign information, political fundraising financials, and legal information within the party. If this information had been leaked, the candidate risked losing credibility within the public eye, being removed from their party affiliation, and being impeached.

As an educator, I managed many students and student issues. By law, the educators and institutions are bound by the Family Educational Rights and Privacy Act of 1974 (FERPA), which protects students' educational histories (Doll, Strein, Jacob, & Prasse, 2011). Research has shown that intentionally violating FERPA with the intent to expose a student's information to other students, faculty, or the world has legal ramifications for the institution, which includes losing their federal funding loss (Essex, 2009; Shellenbarger, & Stearns, 2010) and impairs students academically because students expect that "their personal information [will] be restricted" (McEwan, 2012, p. 18).

I also did extensive scholarly research on conducting a constructivist grounded theory (Charmaz, 2014; Guba, & Lincoln, 1989) study, which included reading and implementing strategies on grounded theory from Charmaz (2014), Creswell (2009), Crotty (1998), and Guba & Lincoln (2001).

Data Collection

Pre-Qualification Interview

Potential study participants expressed their interest to the e-mail address for this study. Potential participants then received information regarding the study, which consisted of the IRB-approved study recruitment poster and the informational recruitment Power Point. Participants wishing to proceed in the study clicked on a link listed in the information to make contact and indicate that they wished to participate in the study. I then contacted the potential participant via e-mail to arrange a pre-study qualification interview. Potential participants learned that the purpose of this interview was to see if the potential participant met the outlined inclusion criteria to be part of the study.

The pre-study qualification interview took place off-site at a mutually agreed upon location and time. At this meeting, potential participants learned about procedures in place to protect their anonymity. Potential participants received random, computer-generated numbers to be used instead of names. They received an e-mail informing them what their number was if they received an invitation to participate in the study. If they were not selected to be part of the study, their random computer generated number, along with their initial e-mail, would be deleted from the pre-qualification interview file in order to protect their anonymity. The computer generated number consisted of random bytes that were listed in Binary format which were generated through random.org, a web site that creates random computer generated numbers based upon the user's specific details.

Potential participants answered a random series of four questions in order to confirm that the employees with CTS were being truthful about their injuries. The random four questions were geared towards specifics about CTS and CTS coping mechanisms. At the end of the pre-qualification interview, potential participants were informed that they would be contacted via e-mail in 24 hours if they met the outlined inclusion criteria to be part of the study. Potential participants who met the inclusion criteria received consent forms, which outlined specifics of the study and the audio recording procedure. Those who wanted to participate in the study had to sign off on two places on the consent form. The first part of the consent form was the potential participant agreeing to be in the study. The second part of the consent form was the potential participant agreeing to be audio taped. The e-mail also contained information regarding how long the participant had to return the signed consent form, which was 10 days from when he or she received the invitation, along with their random computer-generated number. Participants learned their numbers in the e-mail in order to protect their anonymity, and they would be addressed by it throughout the study.

Interview

Participants in this study had the option to pick the location where the on-site, semi-structured interviews would be conducted. The participants and the researcher faced each other. The audio recording device sat between the researcher and participants on the table during the interview to ensure that all questions and responses were clearly heard. At the start of every semi-structured interview, I stated my name, the date and time the interview was taking place, and the participants' computer generated number. Participants were asked to confirm their computer-generated number, along with their signature on the consent form. At the start of the semi-structured interviews, participants received a copy of the semi-structured questions that would be asked during the interview. Participants learned that they could answer the questions in any order, but they must respond to every question. Participants also learned that my role was not to lead the interview, and I was there to learn about their experience. I took notes during the semi-structured interview in the notebook designated for each specified participant.

End of Interview

The semi-structured interviews lasted between 60 and 90 minutes and varied depending upon the participants' recollection of the experience they were describing. At the end of every semi-structured interview, I collected the copy of the interview questions from the participant, thanked the participant for sharing their experience, and reminded the participant that they agreed at the initial interview that they would not discuss the semi-structured questions or the study with anyone. After the participant acknowledged this statement and verbally agreed not to discuss the semi-structured interview and the study, I shut off the recording device waited until the participant left the room before turning the recording device back on and recording specifics about the interview.

Data Analysis

Data analysis in this study utilized the microanalysis techniques and procedures outlined by Strauss and Corbin (1998). This procedure allows and permits researchers the ability and flexibility to move back and forth between the process of collecting and analyzing data so they can immerse themselves in the participants' experience and thereby contribute to the theoretical model. The general framework utilized for data analysis involved open coding, axial coding, and selective coding.

Open Coding

Open coding is the process of breaking data into smaller chunks to look for reoccurring themes and identifying the constructs that are generated by the data (Pandit, 1996) by asking who, what, when, where, and why. Then, through the "comparative method, reoccurring groups, themes, or incidents are grouped together and given the same conceptual label" (Pandit, 1996, para. 12). In this study, constantly comparing the interview responses against the participants' body language during the semi-structured and open-ended interviews provided information about meaning and categories for the investigated participants Kantianisms. By constantly comparing the participants' spoken statements against their body language, the researcher was able to develop concise theories about the psychological, psychosomatic, and sociological effects CTS produces in the workplace.

Axial Coding

The purpose of axial coding is to uniquely put back together data that was separated during open coding to reveal categories, subcategories, and their relationships to each other. Strauss and Corbin (1998) argued that it is the identification and combination of these categories, subcategories, and their relationship to each other which can be used to validate aspects of the developing theory that were not initially revealed by the participants.

Selective Coding

Selective coding is integrating the categories, subcategories, and their relationships in order "to form the initial theoretical framework" (Pandit, 1996. para. 12) within the study. Through selective coding, the participants' words and actions depicted a story, which revealed an insider's perspective on how CTS affected employees on psychological, psychosomatic, and sociological levels both in and out of the RTW program and within their personal lives. Once the core categories and their relationships to each other were identified, a hypothesis was formed based on the relationships, which revealed the invariable nature societal influence has on this disease.

Validity and Reliability

Four different techniques confirmed this study's validity: (a) semi-structured and opened-ended interviews, (b) peer reviewed journal articles, (c) case studies, (d) phenomenological studies, (e) interviews with professionals in occupational therapy, (f) triangulation, and (g) confirming assumptions and hypothesis with participants.

Semi-structured interviews took place consistently for a period of two months, and follow-up open-ended interviews took place approximately for one month. During these three months, both the semi-structured and open-ended interviews were audio recorded and the participants' body language was noted in order to reaffirm the participants' statements. The observations of the participants' body language served as the foundation for creating the open-ended interview questions, which aimed to gain a deeper understanding of the participants' experience with CTS in the workplace, in the RTW, and in their personal lives.

Peer-reviewed journal articles, case studies, and phenomenological studies served to compare and contrast the statements made by the participants. The peer-reviewed journal articles, case studies, and phenomenological studies also provided the exposition and foundation for this study because no studies existed that specifically addressed the rationale and motivation behind the behavior of people with CTS within an RTW program. Peer-reviewed journal articles provided insight into people's feelings about having CTS or about returning to work after being off for an extended period of time with CTS. Case studies on CTS centralized around three aspects of the disease: (a) what CTS was and how the employee contracted it (Prime et al., 2010; Tick, 2013; Vaught, Brismee, Dedrick, Sizer, & Sawyer, 2011); (b) how long it took the employee to return to work and assessed their job performance (Hammond & Harriss, 2012; Jerosch-Herold, Shepstone, Wilson, Dyer, & Blake, 2014; Persson et al., 2014; Tinhofer, Draxler, & Koller, 2013); and (c) focused on employees with CTS' fears (Jenkins, Watts, Duckworth, & McEachan, 2012; Smith-Young, Solberg, & Gaudine, 2014). Phenomenological studies emphasized the employees' fear of the unknown (Hammond & Harriss, 2012; Smith-Young et al, 2014) and how they contend with their fears (Hammond & Harriss, 2012; Smith-Young et al., 2014; Vaught et al., 2011). Research showed that employees' fears centralized around future employability prospects (Murad et al., 2013; O'Rourke, 2014; Parenteau et al., 2011) and the ability to meet financial obligations (Jenkins, Watts, Duckworth, & McEachan, 2012; Murad et al., 2013; O'Rourke, 2014; Smith-Young et al., 2014).

Interviews with professionals in occupational therapy provided training and treatment methods, along with insight and treatment methodologies for treating people with CTS. Interviews with professionals in occupational therapy, along with the peer-reviewed journals, articles, case studies, and phenomenological studies, provided triangulation for data and supporting evidence in this study. Participants confirmed the preliminary interpretations and hypotheses to ensure their accuracy and credibility for observations, findings, and interpretations to prevent over interpreting and miscategorizing the participants' information (Creswell, 2009; Strauss & Corbin, 1998).

Ethical Considerations

One concern raised by this study is that the participants were socio-culturally vulnerable because of the stigmas associated with this disease. The ethical considerations taken into account before every semi-structured and open-ended interview were (a) the effects the interview reflections could have on the participant and (b) the employee with CTS feels additional psychological stress because they are reflecting about the disease and its effects.

Effects

Research showed there is a gamut of emotions that employees with CTS go through (Waylett-Rendall & Niemeyer, 2004) because in addition to dealing with the symptoms of CTS, the employee is also faced with the probability of having to change careers and the necessity of continuing to meet their financial obligations (Dale et al., 2003, Faucett et al., 2000). Therefore, at the start of every semi-structured interview and open-ended interview, participants confirmed their computer generated number and their signature on the consent form. During the semi-structured interviews, participants received a copy of the questions that would be asked during the interview. Participants learned that they could answer the questions in any order, but they must respond to every question. Also, participants knew that at any time if they felt uncomfortable, they could stop the interview.

Participants also learned during the open-ended interviews that they would not receive a copy of the questions because the interview questions were based on their actions and reactions to the semi-structured interview questions. Participants knew that the actions and reactions might create additional open-ended questions and in order to utilize a conversational format, the questions and answers had to come naturally. Participants were also informed that at any time if they felt uncomfortable, they could stop the interview.

Psychological Stress

Research showed that the psychological effects of CTS are both mentally and physically draining on its victims (Idris et al., 2014; Koukoulaiki, 2013; Niedhammer et al., 2010), because CTS causes a downward spiral of psychological, psychosomatic, and sociological "activating events" (Roscigno, Hodson, Lopez, 2009b, p. 729) over which its victims have no control. Research showed this spiral becomes mentally and physically draining on employees with CTS because they are constantly trying to minimize and control the effects of the psychological, psychosomatic, and sociological activating events in order to maintain some form of normalcy in their lives. Studies showed that eventually the psychological and psychosomatic symptoms manifest themselves physically in the employee with CTS (Persson et al., 2014; Sullivan et al., 2013) and have been shown to increase and intensify the effects of stress, anxiety, and hopelessness (Idris et al., 2014; Lallukka et al., 2013; Salo et al., 2010). Psychological and physical exhaustion is the result when the person feels constantly stressed and does not having the opportunity to disengage from the stress (Jacobsen et al., 2014; Lallukka et al., 2013; Mug Kang et al., 2011; Salo, et al., 2010). Studies showed that the effects from activating events eventually crept into every facet of the employee with CTS' personal lives (Kronstrom et al., 2011; Mug Kang et al., 2011). They caused the employee with CTS to experience more stressful effects, which increased the employees' sick days, reduced their productivity even further, and caused additional work stress.

Summary

Patton (2002) argued the predominate goal of qualitative research is for researchers to submerge themselves into a social setting in an attempt to reveal its idiosyncrasies and complexities. Patton argued that researchers have to do this in order to learn the who, what, when, where, why and to what extent the phenomena physically, psychologically, and sociologically exists within each other, why they exist this way, and why they are socially accepted to exist this way. Chapter 3 described the constructivist grounded theory as applied in this study.

Through the use of constructivist grounded theory, participants used their voices and actions to depict their interpretation of the essence and influence CTS had physically, psychologically, psychosomatically, and sociologically in the workplace. In this chapter, participants also discussed their coping mechanisms and their rationalization behind why they used the coping mechanisms they did. Participants revealed in their open-ended interviews that their coping mechanisms helped them to feel normal again and to be accepted by society. This phenomenon is consistent with grounded theory, which states the voices of the participants must be utilized and remain intact in order to accurately describe the problem and the context in which the problem occurred to accurately generate a theory that is specific to an individual's social existence (Creswell, 2009).

In this chapter, data was presented through an extensive discussion of the study's methodology and its relationship to the study's design, participant selection, data collection methods, and analysis. Empirical literature provided comparison and contrast to the statements made by the employees with CTS in this study in order to ensure the study's reliability and validity. The discussion surrounding this study's design ended with a colloquy about the steps employed to reduce psychological stress for the participants in this study.

Chapter 4 discusses this study's findings, themes that repeatedly emerged, and their relevance and significance to answering the research questions. The participants' own words provided insight into the physical, psychological, psychosomatic, and sociological aspects of the social existence and non-acceptance of CTS in the workplace. Findings in this study showed that in addition to the physical limitations that CTS imposes, it also causes strong psychological, sociological, and psychosomatic effects that must be dealt with if the employee with CTS is to fully heal from the effects of this disease.

CHAPTER 4

Results

The intended goal of this study was to provide insight and generate theories about how the physical, social, and emotional effects of carpal tunnel syndrome (CTS), affect employees with CTS' ability to complete an employer-sponsored Return to Work (RTW) program at their place of employment. Through the use of a constructivist grounded theory that utilized Strauss and Corbin's (1998) microanalysis techniques, employees with CTS shared their experience through semi-structured interviews, observations, and open-ended interview questions, which were later used to create meaning. This study consisted of 12 people (five men and seven women) in three separate companies in the United States of America. Participants in this study were recruited through advertisements at local physical rehabilitation centers, hospitals, doctor offices, chiropractic offices, alternative medicine offices, grocery stores, and on social-media pages that were specific to carpal tunnel syndrome. Advertisements contained the first name of the researcher and the e-mail address that was specifically set up for this study so participants could directly contact the researcher.

This chapter will discuss (a) information about this study and the researcher's involvement, (b) description of the participant sample, (c) the research methodology, (d) how the research methodology was applied during data analysis, (e) data analysis, (f) theories that emerged from the data, and (g) summary of the study's findings.

The Study and the Researcher's Involvement

Creswell (2012), Patton (2002), Guba and Lincolin (2001), and Charmaz (2014) made the argument that researchers are considered instruments within the study because they are the ones who will directly interact with the study participants, collect and analyze the study data, and draw theories and conclusions based upon "the process of disassembling and reassembling the data in the development of the emergent theory" (Strauss & Corbin, 1998, p. 128). Patton (2002) and Creswell (2012) further argued that in order for the researcher to be an effective instrument in the study, the exposition relating to the researcher's interest, background, training, past history, participant involvement, and data collection have to be addressed in order to establish credibility, validity, and reduce the opportunity for bias within the study (Creswell, 2012; Patton, 2002).

I became interested in the effects of CTS after personal experience with it in the workplace. In 2005, I was diagnosed with CTS, and within a week of reporting my injury to my manager, I was fired from my position. According to the human resources department, "You are no longer capable of doing the job you were hired to do." It took me three months to find another job, and I spent the next two years fighting the insurance company for my medical bills, which totaled many thousands of dollars, to be paid. The first day at my new job, I hesitated to put on my brace, fearful of quickly being let go. When asked why I was wearing it, I lied. Until 2009, this was how I handled the situation. When I was asked by anyone at work why I wore a brace, I responded with "preventative maintenance." To add legitimacy to my statement, I added some medical terminologies to explain my rationale, and once I saw they were very confused by what I was saying, I knew they would not ask me again. Before seeking alternative medical treatments in 2009, this was my life.

In order to reduce the risk of bias in this study, I concentrated study efforts on aspects of the disease that I had not personally known or experienced. Thus, I chose the Return to Work aspect of this study. I was fired from an organization that did not have a RTW program. The only form of rehabilitation I was offered at the hospital was a sheet of paper that showed how to do wrist exercises a wrist splint. I was left on to heal on my own and deal with psychological and psychosomatic aspect of this disease, which included the lack of a supportive network at home.

My own experience with CTS served as the motivation to continue researching that topic. However, the lack of scholarly research concerning the effects of CTS in the workplace made me wonder if CTS was now a much bigger problem in the workplace than what I personally experienced years ago. Strauss and Corbin's (1998) "seven point criterion checklist" (Kenealy, 2008, para. 22) helped me avoid contaminating the research with personal experience. This checklist stated, "criteria should not be read as hard and fast evaluative rules but merely as guidance, accepting that new areas of investigation may require modification to fit the circumstances" (para. 22). Strauss and Corbin's (1998) checklist, used in conjunction with semi-structured interviews, observations, and field notes, contributed to the creation of individualized open-ended interview questions that were specific to the individual employees' psychological, psychosomatic, and social experience with CTS in the workplace.

Through member checking, participants individually confirmed the preliminary interpretations and hypothesis on a case-by-case basis in order (a) to ensure their accuracy and credibility,(b) to prevent over interpreting and miscategorizing of the participants' information (Creswell, 2009; Strauss & Corbin, 1998), and (c) to highlight any research bias (Strauss & Corbin, 1998) that was not found during the analyzing of the data.

Description of the Sample

Constructivist grounded theory provided the methodological framework for investigating the research questions because of the individuality each participant's experience brought to the study. Individuals were eligible to be part of this study based upon their personal experience with CTS, which must have included (a) contracting CTS because of their job, (b) missing extended periods of work—or having returned to work within the last 45 days—because their CTS needed time to heal, (d) having been diagnosed by a licensed physician, and (e) being under the age of 55.

Theoretical sampling was consistent with constructivist grounded theory and appropriate for this study because it required the participants in this study to be able to recall specifics about their injury, the treatment they received within their employers' RTW programs, and how their co-workers treated them after they returned to work. Through the participants' thoughts, feelings, emotions, and fears, individual stories emerged, which provided insight into the social existence and non-acceptance this disease has in the workplace. Through the use of the employees with CTS' words and experiences, specifics about the physical, psychological, psychosomatic, and sociological experiences helped in the construction of preliminary theories that showed how the cause and effect reactions were the motivating factors of why employees with CTS did or did not complete their employers' RTW programs (Maxwell, 2012; Merriam, 2009; Ritchie et al., 2013).

The sample for this study consisted of five men and seven women, and data collection took place over a three-month period. Nine out of 12 participants' interviews took place in person; three of the interviews took place via Skype because the participants could not travel to meet for an interview. Participants in this study answered semi-structured and open-ended interview questions about their experience with CTS in the workplace, how they dealt with having CTS in the workplace, how they were treated in and out of the RTW program by their employer and co-workers, and why they felt their disease had a direct impact on how they were treated by their employer and co-workers. Observations, in conjunction with the semi-structured interviews, served to confirm or question the participants' responses. Observations also shaped the open-ended interview questions.

The researcher's preliminary interpretations and hypothesis were confirmed on a case-by-case basis by nine of the 12 participants. Because complete anonymity was guaranteed to participants in this study, only demographic information that is pertinent to this study and its findings are provided in Table 1.

Table 1. *Participant Demographic Information*

Participant Number	Gender	Time with CTS	Time at Job	Time in RTW Program
P1	M	10 M	1 Y	8 W
P2	M	2 Y	3 Y	6 W
P3	F	1 Y	11 M	3 W

P4	M	1 Y	7 Y	1 W
P5	F	3 Y	5 Y	5 W
P6	F	2 Y	2 Y	2 M
P7	F	4 M	2 Y	1 M
P8	F	1 Y	4 Y	3 M
P9	F	5 M	7 Y	3 M
P10	F	1 Y	3 Y	2 M
P11	M	2 Y	3 Y	1 M
P12	M	2 Y	6 Y	4 M

Note: Y = Years, M = Months, W = Weeks.

Research Methodology Applied to Data Analysis

Data analysis in this study utilized the microanalysis techniques and procedures outlined by Strauss and Corbin (1988). I began this process by collecting data through semi-structured interviews and observations. Semi-structured interviews, observation notes, and open-ended research questions were kept in a notebook that was color-specific to the participants' computer-generated number. I transcribed and compared interview notes against the audio recordings of the semi-structured interviews and open-ended interviews to ensure their accuracy. Interview notes and audio recordings were then compared against the observation notes to ensure their accuracy. Once the notes and interviews' accuracy were confirmed, I kept two copies of the transcripts and one copy of the audio files.

In order to protect all data, I stored an electronic copy of the transcript on a portable jump drive that was exclusive to one participant. The flash drive was color-coded to match the notebook and the computer generated number for that participant. The portable jump drive was password protected and the password was individually user-specific. Audio files were kept on the same jump drive, which was kept in a locked file cabinet. I was the only person with the key. In addition, I stored the second copy of the transcript, a printed copy, along with printed transcriptions of audio files, in a color-coded folder that was specific to each participant. The participant-specific folders containing the printed transcript of the interviews, observations, and audio recordings were stored in a locked file cabinet in my home office. Only I have the key to this file cabinet. Finally, all original copies of participants' semi structured interview question responses, observation notes, open-ended interview questions, and audio recordings were kept in a locked safe in the researcher's home. When the files were not in use, the files were kept in the locked safe.

Presentation of Data and Results

Data analysis in this study utilized the microanalysis techniques and procedures outlined by Strauss and Corbin (1988). This procedure allows and permits researchers the ability and flexibility to move back and forth between the process of collecting and analyzing data so they can immerse themselves in the participants' experience and thereby contribute to the theoretical model. The general framework for data analysis involved open coding, axial coding, and selective coding to fully illustrate the participants' experiences. According to the guidelines of Strauss and Corbin (1988), each coding process will be presented sequentially and utilize direct excerpts from the participant interviews in order to provide validity for the study categories, subcategories, and theories that emerged.

Open Coding

Open coding is the process of breaking data into smaller chunks to look for reoccurring themes and identify the constructs that are generated by the data (Pandit, 1996) by asking who, what, when, where, and why. Then, through the "comparative method, reoccurring groups, themes, or incidents are grouped together and given the same conceptual label" (Pandit, 1996, para. 12). In this study, constantly comparing the interview responses against the participants' body language during the semi-structured and open-ended interviews contributed to the search for meaning and helped in the development of categories for the participants' Kantianisms. By constantly comparing the participants' spoken statements against their body language, I was able to develop theories about the psychological, psychosomatic, and sociological effects CTS produces in the workplace. Data saturation was reached after six interviews because no new ideas or supporting evidence emerged. During open coding, 19 concepts were coded. The 19 coded concepts, along with direct quotations from participants and interpretations of their body language supporting the 19 concepts are listed in Appendix B.

Axial Coding

The purpose of axial coding is to uniquely put back together data that was separated during open coding to reveal categories and subcategories and their relationships to each other. Strauss and Corbin (1998) argued that it is the identification and combination of these categories, subcategories, and their relationship to each other that can be used to validate aspects of the developing theory that were not initially revealed by the study's participants. The constant comparison process allowed analysis of the concepts that were generated during open coding against the categories and subcategories that emerged during axial coding. Once the relationships between the concepts and categories were revealed, the categories and subcategories could be compared against each other in order to reveal their inner working relationships.

Within the 19 identified concepts that the qualitative software program, NVivo revealed, six categories repeatedly emerged that gave insight into the psychological, psychosomatic, and sociological effects of CTS within the workplace. Within the six categories, three to five subcategories emerged, and these were used to provide further insight into these effects. Each of the categories and their corresponding subcategories are listed in their respective tables and figures, along with the corresponding research question that they answered. Table 2 lists the psychological categories and subcategories found during axial coding. Figure 1 depicts a graphical representation of the psychological categories and subcategories found during axial coding. Research Questions 2 and 3 will be discussed in this section. Table 3 lists the psychosomatic categories and subcategories that were found in axial coding. Figure 2 depicts a graphical representation of the psychosomatic categories and subcategories found during axial coding. Research Question 5 will be discussed in this section. Table 4 lists the sociological categories and subcategories that were found in axial coding. Figure 3 depicts a graphical representation of the sociological categories and subcategories found during axial coding. Research Question 1 will be discussed in this section. A detailed description of the categories, subcategories, and direct quotes from the participant interviews follows each table.

Psychological aspects. RQ2. How much impact does an injured employee's psychological makeup have on how well he or she will perform at his or her job after returning from a work place injury?

Employees with CTS' psychological makeups were shown to have a direct impact on their work performance based upon their feelings of being helpless to stop the effects of this disease in taking over their professional lives. Throughout their semi-structured and open-ended interviews, employees with CTS repeatedly conveyed and showed their frustrations and impatience with the limiting effects of this disease by comparing their current work situations to their past work situations. Employees with CTS specifically reflected on things they could no longer do in their interviews. Their body language echoed their frustration and impatience with this disease as they were unable to sit still during their interviews and became agitated when reflecting upon their past abilities.

Employees with CTS also revealed that their physical limitations added to their sensitivity and heightened their psychological and sociological awareness to their surroundings when they were asked about their injury by their employer and co-workers. Employees with CTS discussed in their interviews how CTS affected and diminished their work performance to the extent that they repeatedly feared losing their job on a semi-regular basis. More than one employee with CTS admitted in their open-ended interviews that their repeated fear of losing their job heightened tensions between themselves, their employer and coworkers, and contributed to their declining performance at work.

RQ3. How do the effects of employers' bias towards employees with CTS affect the employee's successful completion rate of a RTW program?

Employees with CTS' psychological makeup were shown to have a direct impact on their work performance because of the psychological factors employees with CTS associated with their employers' response to their disease. During their open-ended interviews, employees with CTS reported feeling diminished to their co-workers due to the non-verbal communication their employers displayed when employees with CTS were limited in their abilities due to the effects of CTS. Employees with CTS also reported feeling distressed, awkward, and discomfited about having to wear their braces or stretch openly in public because of the comments or looks their employers gave them.

Psychological stress was prominent in employees with CTS' open-ended interviews. Employees with CTS interpreted the non-verbal communication that their employers displayed towards their disease and their limited abilities as the employers' feeling they were more of hindrance than an asset to the organization and repeatedly feared losing their job because of it. Employees with CTS stated that the fear of job loss occupied a good portion of their day, which indirectly made them doubt and question their abilities to perform in a satisfactory manner, as well as significantly contributed to a decline and interfered with their work day performance on a regular basis.

Table 2. Psychological

Category	Subcategories	Additional Themes
Helplessness	Emotional	Anger
		Frustration
		Sadness and Fear
	Physical	
	Mental	Loss of Control
		Job Stability
		Emotional Stability
		Social Isolation

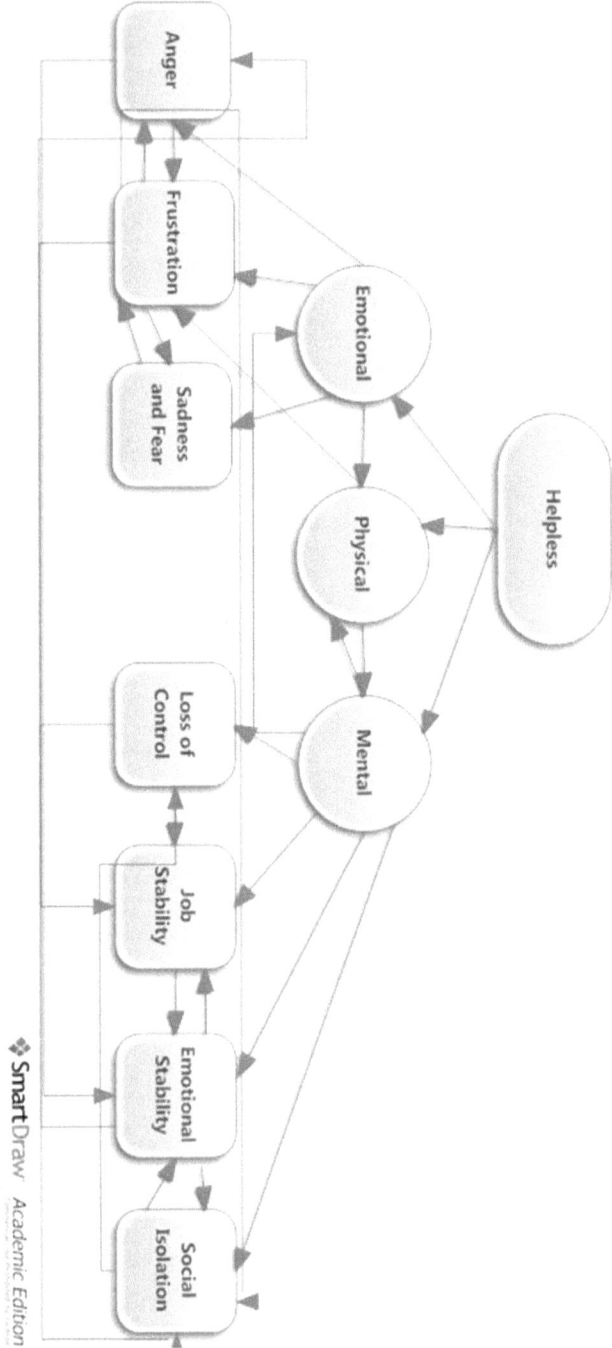

Figure 1. Axial coding: Psychological.

Helplessness. Helplessness was the first theme to emerge consistently amongst the participants in this study regarding their CTS. Specifically, participants described and referred to their current work situation and their ability to keep their job as feeling helpless and unable to stop their employer from terminating their employment. Some example interview statements follow:

> CTS to me means I will forever have to wear this stupid brace and eventually lose my job. I'm forever going to be different. How do you not just give up? (P1)

> I worked day and night to get this promotion and I feel it was all for nothing now. Every day as I leave to go to the RTW, I see the temp come in to do my job. Every day I think, how long before they replace me. I look at my wrist and think, my own body did this to me. (P10)

> I feel helpless to stop my boss from firing me. No matter how hard I try, he gives me these looks that tell me that my best just isn't good enough anymore. I can't just fix this problem and just make it go away and that is what I think he wants, for me and my problem to go away. How messed up is that? (P7)

Emotional responses. All of the participants reported feeling emotional at some point of their workday about their illness and reported that it had a direct impact on what they were doing at the given moment. Emotional responses reported by participants were anger, frustration, sadness and fear.

Anger.

> Why did this have to happen to me? I did everything right! I sat straight. My feet were on the floor. I never slouched at my desk when working. Why didn't this happen to the other writer? She has a cheap keyboard. (P3)

I hate this happened to me. I hate that I'm injured. I hate my boss for letting this happen to me. How could this happen? (P4)

I feel like I've been lied to. I see the looks I get when I walk down the hall. One person in my department that I help train, who used to eat lunch with me, won't even make eye contact with me anymore. I'm so angry. I didn't do this! I didn't ask for this! I'm a good person, damnit! Bad stuff is supposed to happen to bad people. I volunteer, I help others. This ain't right. (P10)

I wish they would just fire me and get it over with! It beats coming in here every day and dealing with the looks and stares from people I thought were my friends. Giving up is easier than putting up with this crap (P12).

Frustration.

I can't do anything anymore! I can't type. I can't code. I can't work. I want to work. (P11)

This sucks! I used to be able to dirt bike ride. Now the vibration brings tears to my eyes cause it hurts so much. (P3)

I just want my normal life back. I miss the life I had. I was so happy. (P6)

Sadness and Fear.

I used to like coming into work. I miss that. Now I can't wait to get out of here after 8 hours. Between the looks and whispers as I come and go out of the program, I just want to go home and leave this place behind me. (P1)

I thought I had the perfect job. Everything about it was perfect. I used to go to training, learned the latest software, and others thought I was great at what I did. Now every day when I walk in I wonder if HR has a box waiting for me on my desk. (P9)

Life before Carpal Tunnel was good. I was this awesome work machine. I could work 12 hour days and come in the next and do it all over again. I was always way ahead of schedule on my projects. Now I'm lucky when my Carpal Tunnel flares up if I can even type. I have this horrible feeling I'm gonna have to choose between my job and my hand. Stuff like this didn't happen to my dad where he worked. Employers cared about you back then. (P8)

I used to like the people I worked with, even my boss was awesome. Now it's all different and messed up here. I get the boring projects and no one talks to me. I just wanna quit. (P5)

Physical impacts. Participants reported that the physical symptoms of CTS had direct impacts in both their work and home life, with each indirectly affecting the other. Examples of physical symptoms were not being physically productive prior to contracting CTS, CTS' physical symptoms, and the effects of the prescribed medications.

It's so hard to do my job now. I used to type 120 words a minute, now there are days when I have to take pain killers just to get through the morning and can barely type 30 words. (P7)

Getting woken up by the dull ache and numbness in my wrist really sucks. I have a hard time getting up in the morning for work now because I don't get a good night's rest. This really impacts my productivity at work too. I find it hard to concentrate and stay alert. Coffee used to help, but there's only so much of that you can drink before getting really bad jitters. (P11)

I don't know which is worse. My wrist hurting, the numbness and tingling, or my stomach being torn up by the pain killers. (P12)

Mental impacts. Participants reported that the psychological effects caused by the combination of co-worker comments and what they viewed as questionable looks from their employers directly affected their workday, because it made them self-conscious about the outward appearance of their disease.

My co-worker once asked me if Harry Houdini knew I had borrowed his device. She was referring to my hand braces. This really made me self-conscious about wearing my braces at work. (P3)

I will never forget the look my boss gave me the first time I put my brace on. Talk about uncomfortable. I quickly put my hand behind my back to hide it. Every time he sees me now, he looks at my hands. It's like he is keeping a tally or something of when I am wearing my brace. (P5)

Wearing my brace at work makes me feel like I'm a freak of nature. I'm constantly reminded of my disease and how it throws up a red flag that I am different than everyone else here. I swear there's a bullseye with my name dead center. (P5)

Loss of Control. Participants discussed feeling they had lost control over their own lives. This included a fear of job loss, which was viewed as a means of stability because it was how they paid their bills, fed their families, purchased items, and funded their retirement. Others discussed loss of control from a mental standpoint.

Job Stability.

My career path was clearly defined. I would completed graduate school and then apply to be a manger within my department. Now because of Carpal Tunnel

Syndrome, I have a hard time holding a pen some days. How the heck am I supposed to be a manager and have people look up to me when I can't even hold a freaking pen. (P12)

I keep thinking how will I survive? All the good paying jobs revolve around computers so unless I want to work in a factory, or push a broom, what the heck am I going to do to pay my bills and live? (P9)

I left home when I was 16 and nothing was given to me. Everything I have I worked hard to get. Now what? It all goes away because of some pain in my wrist? This disease is trying to destroy me from the inside out! (P6)

My daughter needs braces; my son wants to play soccer. That costs money. We are a two-income household. How do I tell my family that they can't have the things they want and still look myself in the mirror? What kind of parent am I? (P4)

Emotional Stability.

I have moments where I just want to run, hide, and cry because I am so ashamed what happened to me. A big part of me was my job, now that's in jeopardy and it isn't my fault. I could understand if I did something to cause this, but I didn't. How do you control something that you can't even see happening? (P8)

The only real sense of control I have right now is taking my meds. When I take my meds, I know I can stop the pain. (P1)

I can't sleep, at least not like I used to. I can't work, not like I used to. I have to use my other hand now as my primary one because it doesn't hurt to use it. I can't help out around the house, because it hurts to wash the floors, or mow the lawn. I feel like a bum. (P5)

I have learned that the only way to control what is happening to me is to not let it beat me. I can't use power tools anymore, so now I have an electric lawn mower. I have to sleep with my brace on, but the pain in my wrist doesn't wake me up anymore, so I do it. I give my wrist a break when I am home by staying off of my computer. If I need something typed up, I ask one of my daughters to do it for me. This seems to help. (P9)

Social Isolation. There was a strong feeling of being socially isolated at work by participants. Participants felt they were purposely being left out of department decisions and were psychologically bullied by their managers, co-workers, or both. Employees reported socially withdrawing from work when the psychological bullying efforts were increased and intensified.

For as long as I can remember we used to have our department meeting every Friday at 9:00am. When I returned to work and entered the return to work program, our department meeting got moved to the same time that I am participating in the program. When I asked my manager about this, he told me not to be such a worrywart. I tried to talk to him about two weeks later and he told me there was nothing going on in the meeting that concerned me and that's why it was moved (P8).

We used to be a really close group. We went to lunch together and even hung out on the weekends sometimes at our kids events. But after I got injured, that all changed. My daughter came home crying because my co-workers daughter said they couldn't play together anymore. When I asked my co-worker about this, she told me how she parents her daughter is none of my business. I was really shocked by this. Over the next few weeks, I noticed that my co-worker had her desk moved away from mine and her interaction with me just stopped. When I tried talking to her about this, she told me I was paranoid. I stopped talking to my co-worker after this. I figured what's the point? (P7)

I got called into Human Resources not too long after I returned from my surgery. I was told my manager complained that I took too long in the bathroom in the morning and took too long making my lunch. Because everyone else worked more than 8 hours a day, I too was expected to do the same. Human Resources told me I would have to stay an extra 15 minutes a day to make up the time. I was asked to sign an agreement about this and I refused. I stayed the extra 15 minutes every day, but my wrist began to hurt more. Eventually I just stopped staying because I couldn't take the pain anymore and the painkillers the doctor gave me were starting to tear my stomach up pretty bad. (P3)

My manager doesn't ask me what I was working on, rather, she asks my co-worker. She does this right in front of me and when I said something once, both my manager and co-worker ignored what I was saying and continued talking about my work right in front of me. I stopped speaking up in meetings after this and tried to go with the flow. (P9)

The only time my manager speaks to me is through e-mail, unless another manager is around in a public area, then she will say good morning to me. If she sees me in the hallway, she quickly turns her eyes away from me. (P6)

My manager read my status report out loud once in front of our entire department. She corrected my grammar in front of everyone. When I spoke to her in private about it afterwards, I was told that it was a learning exercise so everyone could benefit. That was dumbest thing I ever heard. I used to spend hours writing a status report that only used to take me twenty minutes before because I did not want to be publicly made fun of again. (P10)

Psychosomatic aspects. RQ5. How do co-workers psychologically affect an employee with CTS's completion rate in an employer sponsored RTW Program?

Employees with CTS stated their psychological health was directly affected by their co-workers psychosomatically, which means employees with CTS felt physical symptoms that were psychologically related. During their open-ended interviews, employees with CTS stated that the relationship with their co-workers affected them more physically and psychologically than the relationship with their employers because of the day-to-day interactions the employees with CTS had with their co-workers. During their open-ended interviews, employees with CTS reported internalizing the comments their co-workers made to a point to where they became physically ill. Employees with CTS also reported that the combination of the psychological and physical effects were so overwhelming at times that they were physically and mentally unable to perform at their jobs.

Participants revealed in their semi-structured and open-ended interviews that when they experienced negative psychological and sociological interaction, isolation, and comments from their employers and co-workers regarding their injury, they experienced an increase in psychosomatic symptoms that would manifest themselves physically, psychologically, or both. Reoccurring themes found during the interviews were bowel disorders, stress, anxiety, depression, self-induced isolation, and increased sick days. Excerpts highlighting these emotions in the interviews follow and are separated into the categories of physical, psychological, and physical and psychological symptoms combined. Corresponding subcategories are listed underneath each.

Table 3. Psychosomatic

Categories	Subcategories
Physical Symptoms	Bowel Disorders
Psychological Symptoms	Self-Induced Isolation
	Depression
	Anxiety
Physical & Psychological Symptoms	Panic Attacks
	Depression & Anxiety

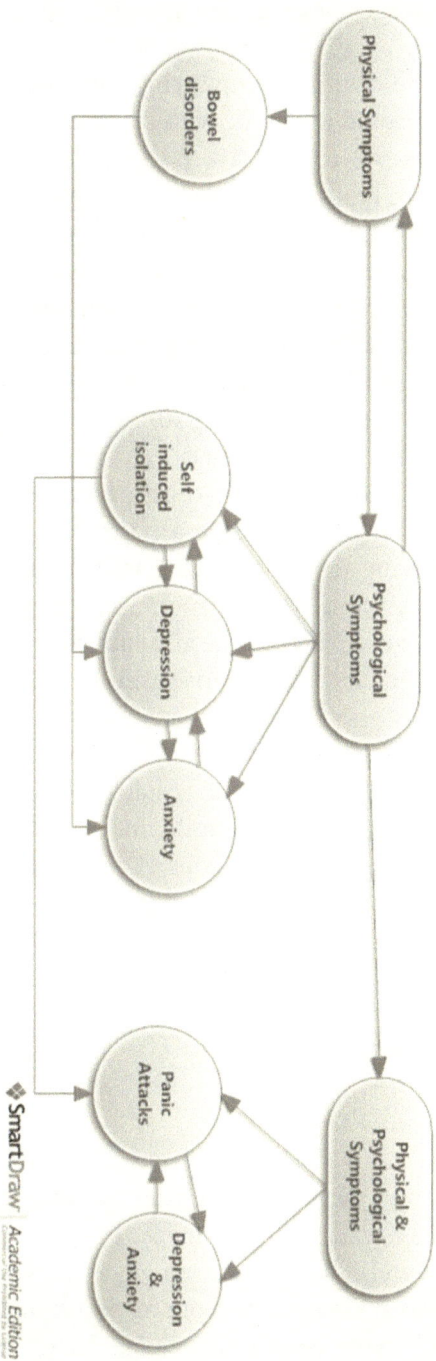

Figure 2. Axial coding: Psychosomatic.

Physical Symptoms. Participants described bowel disorders that resulted from the stress they endured at work.

> Once my boss wrote me up saying I missed my project deadline. I could only type with one hand that day and I let her know that. She asked me what I thought my ability was to be able to continue to do my job. Amazing how me being able to only type with one hand didn't make it into my write up. When it was all over, I was so upset I spent the next 45 minutes in and out of the bathroom. I still can't wrap my head around this. She made it seem like I missed my deadline on purpose. I swear she wants to fire me. (P10)

> I began to notice after the third or fourth time after one of my co-workers made a nasty comment about me not having to work as hard as everyone else does that I can't go to the bathroom. The first time this happened, I used prune juice and suppositories. I ran to the bathroom and I began to spasm. I was scared. (P9)

> To control my bathroom issues, I eat less than I used to. My doctor told me I have Irritable Bowel Syndrome and from what I read, if you do not overeat, then your symptoms are less. I drink tons of water now. When it does flare up, my leg muscles hurt so bad and so does my tummy. I feel like I am walking in slow motion and just to walk is an effort. (P3)

Psychological symptoms.

Self-induced isolation.

> After dealing with question after question about my injury, I just want to be left alone. I used to like going into work and talking to my co-workers. Now, I come in, sit down at my desk, and put my headphones on. It's my way of saying do not disturb me. It's the best way I can think how to deal with all of this. (P9)

I don't talk to anyone any more. I come in, do my job, and go home. I start counting down my eight-hour day the minute my car pulls into the parking lot. (P7)

My co-worker once said to me, you should be able to get these two pages typed before you leave today. Not like I asked you to do something complicated. I felt really deflated by that statement. I did the typing and e-mailed it to her. We used to talk over the cube wall all the time. After that, I didn't want to talk to her anymore. How can you be a team player after that? (P9)

I noticed the effects of my workday creeping into my personal life when I snapped at my husband, and he said, "Don't talk to me the way your boss talks to you." That's when it really hit home for me that I need to find another job and quit. (P7)

Depression.

I don't want to get up in the morning anymore. I just lay there in bed and don't move until the absolute second that I have to. My husband told me to get up and go to work. He just doesn't get it that I just want the world to go away. (P5)

My day used to start with working out and end with working out. I don't work out any more. I just lay around doing nothing. I stare off into space a lot and start crying for no reason. (P5)

I have a really hard time getting out of bed in the morning and falling asleep at night. I wake up in the middle of the night and I can't fall back to sleep. I started taking sleeping pills, but they have stopped working. The only time I actually sleep is on Friday and Saturday because I don't have to go to work the next day. (P11)

I look at my wrist and I think I failed my family. My career is going to end and I have no idea what to do. All I know how to do is write code. Every job out there requires you to use your hands. I can't help out around the house like I used to and my wife is all over me about it. Nothing like feeling like a failure and then being made to feel like you are a failure by someone who promised to love you forever. (P12)

Anxiety.

I can't stop thinking about work. All I do when I get home is relive the events over and over and over again. My stomach is in knots and I can't go to the bathroom. I count my fiber grams and drink fiber shakes. Nothing is helping. I can't sleep on my stomach because it is so bloated now it hurts. My balance is off, too. (P6)

I keep thinking, what ways are my boss and co-workers going to screw with me today to make my life a living hell? I've actually started coming in at 6 a.m. just so I can leave before 3 p.m. and have to deal with them less. The hours without them are wonderful. (P5)

After I got hurt, I started calling in sick. My boss noticed a pattern and asked me what was going on. Before it all came out about my injury, I lied. I was so afraid of being fired that I just made something up. I know he doesn't trust me now because I lied. I always see him watching me while I am working. I screwed my life up and there is nothing I can do about it. My parents were right; always tell the truth. (P3)

Every day the same thought goes through my head on the way to work, is this the day I'm going to get fired? Did they find a way to get rid of me? (P10)

I have a hard time sitting still at my desk. I can't concentrate or focus. I make simple errors and I get written up for it. My boss told me I had better thoroughly check my work before submitting it to her that it would be in my best interest. I know that was a read between the lines statement. She's going to fire me. (P9)

The phone rang the other day shortly after I got home. I was ready to bet money on it that it was the office calling me to tell me not to come in tomorrow. (P12)

I accused my wife of being in cahoots with my employer because she made the comment that the lawn still wasn't mowed. The hurt look in her eyes was more than I could bear at that moment. (P11)

Physical and psychological symptoms.

Panic attacks.

My boss once said to me, ever think about going into another line of work? I just stood there. Later I felt like the walls were closing in on me and I couldn't breathe. I just kept thinking I had to get out of here. I left work early that day. (P5)

I get nauseous as I drive into work. I can feel my stomach swell and I just don't feel good. I dread getting up in the morning. I lay awake at night watching my clock tick away. If I wake up before my alarm, I get depressed because I count the minutes until I have to get up. There are times when I panic about going to work and I come up with an excuse to call in. (P6)

I got a verbal warning about my job performance and all I could think about was, what is going to happen next? The entire scenario played out in my head. I could see myself getting fired. (P10)

Depression and anxiety.

> I get up for work every day and all I can think about is how am I going to make it through the next eight hours? They seem endless. The workdays feel like months. (P11)

> I keep looking at old pictures of myself when I was happy, before I got injured, and I so desperately want to go back to feeling that way. I remember it, but it seems so far away now. (P4)

Sociological aspects. RQ1. How does an employee inflicted with carpal tunnel syndrome's morals, values, and ethics dictate his or her success or failure rate for completing a RTW program?

According to Velasquez (2006), morals, values, and ethics are all intertwined because morals are what a people use to define what they believe is right or wrong. Velasquez further argued that a person takes his or her beliefs about what is right or wrong and assigns worth to them. The worth is what transforms into people's ethics because the assigned worth defines a person's behavior (p. 27).

In their open-ended interviews, employees with CTS repeatedly discussed how they felt they were treated at work by their employers and co-workers. Their acknowledgement that they were treated badly arguably indicated that the employees were able to comprehend the difference between good and bad, right and wrong, acceptable and unacceptable behavior in the workplace. The worth the employees with CTS assigned to their employers' and co-workers' behavior ultimately reflected their feelings about their ethics in this situation and was what made the employees with CTS decide if they would or would not modify their behavior. The feelings expressed in their open-ended interviews revealed that employees with CTS internally struggled with what they believed was right and wrong and what their employer and co-workers insinuated was right or wrong.

Participants revealed in their semi-structured and open-ended interviews that when they experienced negative sociological interaction with their co-workers and employers, their psychological sensitivity to their surroundings and their injury increased. Two reoccurring themes were loss of self-esteem, which directly affected their work day, and waiting for the ineviatable, which encompassed their daily thoughts and fears surrounding job loss. Excerpts highlighting these emotions in the interviews follow and are separated into the categories of loss of self-esteem and waiting for the inevitable. There were no subcategories found by Nvivo in this area.

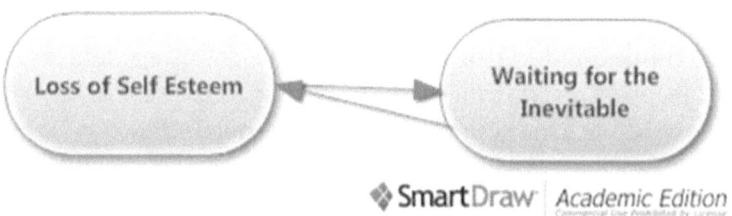

Figure 3. Axial coding: Sociological.

Loss of self-esteem.

I have no self-confidence any more when it comes to work. I feel so beaten down. My co-worker said to me the other day, "Why don't you just quit, not like you do anything here worthwhile anyway." I thought about going to HR with this, but then I was like, what's the point, they didn't help me the last five times I reported stuff like this, and it got turned around on me anyway, and I was told to be a better team player. (P5)

One of the worst statements ever said to me by my co-worker, "Can you show me how to do your job?" I couldn't help but think the writing was on the wall. (P6)

I had a disagreement with my boss once; he said to me, "Do you want to get fired today? Then get back to your desk and write." I went back to my desk and updated my profile on the local job board. I knew he would fire me given the opportunity. I quickly re-financed my home and car just to be on the safe side and started stock piling food. (P10)

My boss told me my work was unacceptable and stood across from me with her finger pointed at my chair and said, "Sit down there and write!" I felt like a dog being commanded to sit. (P7)

Nothing like walking into a room and people stop talking. If it only happened once or twice, I wouldn't think anything of it, but I started counting, and it happens every time now. I saw someone point at my wrist once, hard not to take that personal. (P8)

I feel bullied. I never get told what I did right at work; all I hear is what I did wrong. My boss pulls me into meetings just as the office is filling up so when our meeting is over, everyone can see us walking out of the conference room, and it's not like our meetings are quiet either. The conference room is known as the you-are-in-trouble room at work, too. (P1)

Waiting for the inevitable.

I've been written up so many times at work now I've lost count. I never get a copy so I never get to see my statements in writing. If they want to fire me, why don't they just do it and stop screwing with my head? (P12)

A co-worker told me that they think my boss is trying to fire me. Then he said, "I will miss you." How the heck are you supposed to respond to that! It's not like I could talk to HR about what he said to me, much less my boss. (P9)

I was once told that I needed to pull my weight more in the department by a co-worker and stop using my injury as an excuse to get out of working overtime. (P3)

My co-worker constantly talks over me at meetings when I am speaking. My boss always takes her side and tells me to lower my voice when I try to get a word in edge wise. (P5)

The company wanted everyone to work overtime in order to get our product out the door on time. Because of my injury, I can't. A lady in payroll saw me leaving and said, "Why do you get to leave?" My boss just stood there and let the payroll chick ream me out. (P7)

My boss talks to everyone in our department but me. When I ask for help with something, she tells me to e-mail her so she has a written record of it. She doesn't do this with my other co-workers. I talked to her boss about it and nothing was ever done about it. I tried talking to HR about it, but after my third request I just gave up. (P9)

Selective Coding

Selective coding is integrating the categories, subcategories, and their relationships in order "to form the initial theoretical framework" (Pandit, 1996, para. 12) within this study. Through selective coding, the participants' words and actions depicted a story, which revealed an insider's perspective on how CTS affected employees on psychological, psychosomatic, and sociological levels both in and out of the RTW program and within their personal lives. Once the core categories and their relationships to each other were identified, observation notes validated the participants' interview responses. According to Strauss and Corbin (1988), validating the relationships between categories is important in data analysis because it reaffirms that the researcher has accurately selected the predominant research category. Findings from this study showed there was a direct relationship to the influence society can have on the effects of CTS through psychological, psychosomatic, and sociological actions (Figure 4).

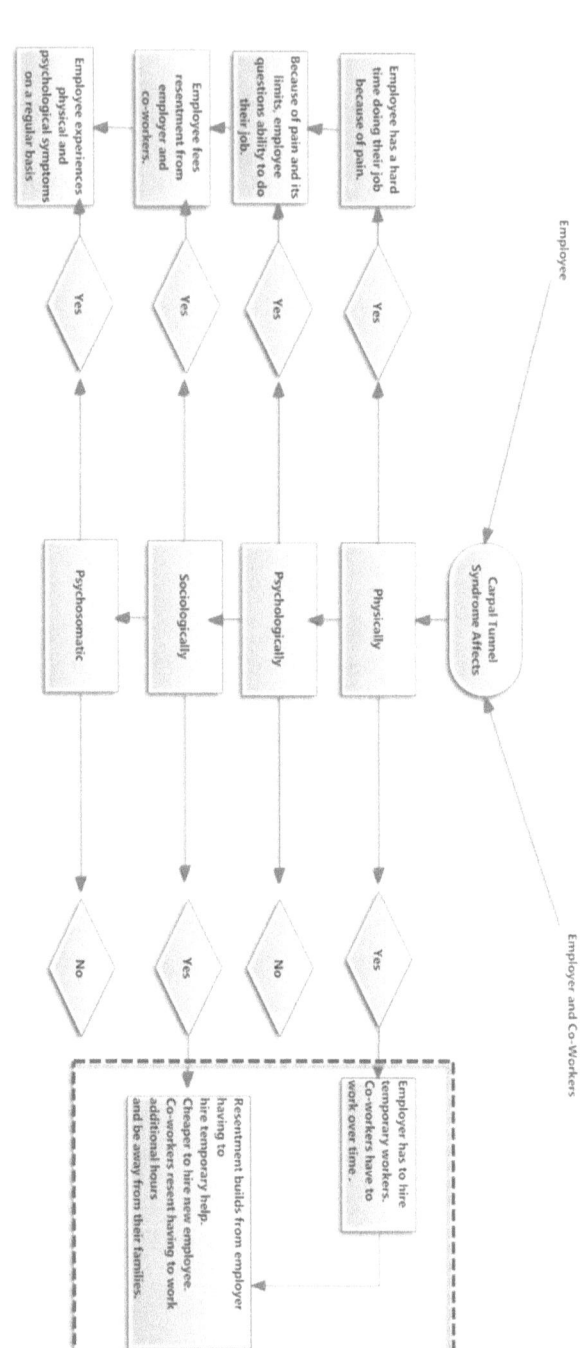

Figure 4. Conditional/consequential matrix.

Member Checking

The researcher utilized Strauss and Corbin's (1988) member checking, which states the best way to ensure that the participants' information was gathered and analyzed correctly is to ask the participants to "read it and then request that they comment on how well it seems to fit their cases" (p. 159). Following analysis, the participants received an e-mailed containing their individual statements, the axial coding scheme, and the conditional/consequential matrix. Participants commented on the accuracy of the collection of their individual statements and observations, along with providing feedback on how they felt the researcher related their experience to having CTS in the workplace. Participants had five days to complete this task, and if they wished to opt out, they could let the researcher know within 24 hours. Nine participants responded, and Table 5 displays their comments. One participant opted out, and two participants did not respond to the request.

Table 4. *Member Check: Participants' Comments*

Number	Statement
P2	I'm not crazy! I thought I was going crazy! Every minute of my day seems to revolve around this stupid disease. I'm not the only one! I feel a bit better now.
P10	You mean this is normal to feel this way? Two of my co-workers told me I was nuts and that I should just quit. I felt horrible when they said that to me. I actually began thinking they were right.
P5	Thank you. It's nice to know I am not alone out here.
P1	I read what you wrote and I cried. This is my life and finally someone besides me gets it. The frustration is overwhelming. I wasn't raised like this. I keep telling myself to be strong, but it's so hard.

P12	So I'm not the only one who feels this way at work? You mean this goes on at other places too! This ain't right. Something and someone needs to stop this. I have a wife and kids. They shouldn't be subjected to this just because I'm hurt. Who gives anyone the right to judge me!
P9	I almost handed in my resignation the other day. I was ready to. I swear I was. Then I saw your e-mail and read my comments and looked at the graphic and it all clicked! I knew I could do something after reading your e-mail. Thank you.
P4	You were dead on! Every emotion I was feeling came out in my statement. I could hear myself saying what you wrote and I was like, finally, finally someone else gets it.
P6	I read what you wrote and for the first time since all of this started I went to work and my stomach didn't hurt. It was like this huge weight was lifted.
P3	I admit I quit my job. I couldn't take it anymore. But at least now I know it all wasn't me. I'm still trying to deal with all of this, but at least now I know it all wasn't me.

Summary

Twelve people took part in a study that sought to examine the psychological, psychosomatic, and sociological effects of CTS in the workplace. Through the use of a constructivist grounded theory methodology, participants in this study answered semi-structured and open-ended interview questions about their experience with CTS in the workplace, how they dealt with having CTS in the workplace, how they were treated in and out of the RTW program by their employer and co-workers, and why they felt their disease had a direct impact on how they were treated by their employer and co-workers. Observations, in conjunction with the semi-structured interviews, confirmed or enhanced the participants' responses. Observations also guided the creation of the open-ended interview questions.

The employees with CTS' words and experiences helped to answer the research questions:

> RQ1. How does an employee afflicted with carpal tunnel syndrome's morals, values, and ethics dictate his or her success or failure rate for completing a RTW program?

> RQ2. How much impact does an injured employee's psychological makeup have on how well he or she will perform at his or her job after returning from a workplace injury?

> RQ3. How do the effects of employer's bias towards employees with CTS affect the employee's successful completion rate of a RTW program?

> RQ4. How does an employer's morals, values, and ethics dictate whether he or she will implement a RTW program for employees inflicted with CTS?

> RQ5. How do co-workers psychologically affect an employee with CTS's completion rate in an employer-sponsored RTW Program?

Results of this study provided physical, psychological, psychosomatic, and sociological insight into the social existence and non-acceptance of this disease in the workplace.

This chapter presented the findings of the data analysis techniques that were used in this study and revealed an insider's perspective on how CTS affected employees on psychological, psychosomatic, and sociological levels both in and out of the RTW program and within their personal lives. In the following chapter, the significance of this study's findings, along with a discussion about the study's findings compared to present literature surrounding this topic will be discussed. Chapter 5 will also discuss the limitations found in this study and present future recommendations for further research surrounding this topic.

CHAPTER 5

Discussion, Implications, Recommendations

Introduction

Chapter 5 discusses the significance of this study's findings and is separated into three sections. Section 1 reiterates the study's findings and discusses their significance in terms of the original research questions and the methodology used to create this study. Section 2 discusses the study's findings and how well they fit with present literature surrounding the study topic. Included in this discussion is a comparison of the categories and theories, which emerged in this study and how they are or are not compatible with findings from past studies. Section 3 discusses the limitations of this study and presents recommendations for future research in this area.

Findings of the Study

The purpose of the research questions for this study were aimed at identifying the reasons why an employee with CTS does or does not complete his or her employer-sponsored RTW program. Through the use of a constructivist grounded theory approach, which consisted of semi-structured interviews, open-ended interviews, and observations, the employees with CTS' own words helped to reveal the essence and influence that the physical, psychological, psychosomatic, and sociological aspects of CTS have on each other and how they influence an employee's day-to-day physical and psychological workplace activities. Past studies and literature provided the exposition for this study.

Data analysis in this study utilized the microanalysis techniques and procedures outlined by Strauss and Corbin (1988) and consisted of (a) open coding, (b) axial coding, and (C) selective coding. Open coding was used to break the data into smaller chunks and look for reoccurring themes. Axial coding was used to put the data back together, which helped identify categories, subcategories, and their relationships to each other. Selective coding provided the foundation for the "initial theoretical framework" (Pandit, 1996, para. 12) within this study and revealed an insider's perspective on how CTS affected employees with CTS on psychological, psychosomatic, and sociological levels both in and out of the RTW program and within their personal lives. Study findings were confirmed and validated by nine of the 12 study participants using Strauss and Corbin's (1988) technique of member checking in order to ensure their accuracy and credibility.

Relevance of the Findings to the Literature

The findings in this study are aligned with case studies and phenomenological studies examining and determining the effects of CTS in the workplace. Through the use of the sociological biopsychosocial (BPS) model, this study directly contributes to the current body of knowledge surrounding the effects of CTS in the workplace because it fills in the missing gaps of previous case studies and phenomenological studies that measured one or two aspects of this disease. The BPS model proved relevant in this study because it provides the necessary framework to show how the employees with CTS' physical, psychological, psychosomatic, and sociological experiences and struggles are intertwined and are as unique and individualized (Walker, Jackson, & Littlejohn, 2004) as the participants in this study.

The core concepts that emerged from this study were consistent with present day literature surrounding this topic in both case studies and phenomenological studies. The six core concepts found in this study, (a) helplessness (Clay & Olitt, 2012; Glasø, Vie, Holmadal, & Einarsen, 2011; Sloan et al., 2010; Stojanova, 2014), (b) physical symptoms (Egan et al., 2009; Nixon et al., 2011; Persson et al., 2014; Shoss & Shoss, 2012; Sullivan et al., 2013), (c) psychological symptoms (Anderson et al., 2012; Banerjee et al., 2014; McFarlane, 2013), (d) physical and psychological symptoms (Koukoulaiki, 2013; Lavie-Ajayi et al., 2012; ; Law et al., 2011; Mug Kang et al., 2011), (e) loss of self-esteem (MacIntosh, 2012; Martin & Martin, 2010; Martin, & LaVan, 2010; McCormack et al., 2009; McFarlane, 2013; Miranda et al., 2009), and (f) waiting for the inevitable (Cho et al., 2012; Egan et al., 2009) provided insight into the psychological, psychosomatic, and sociological effects of CTS within the workplace. The remainder of this section will discuss how this study contributed to the current body of knowledge surrounding the effects of CTS in the workplace.

Helplessness

Helplessness describes the psychological state that employees felt having CTS and dealing with their CTS symptoms in and out of the RTW program and within their personal lives. Current studies and findings in this study all support this category and its subcategories of emotional, physical, and mental impacts. The additional categories within the subcategories of emotional and mental impacts were also consistent with the BSP model, thereby indicating that the emotions and experiences are all intertwined.

The differences between previous qualitative studies and this study were the focal point of the participant's experience and how it was used to generate and interpret data to indicate the feelings of helplessness the employees with CTS felt. Case studies examined the effects of CTS by recruiting participants who met their study's guidelines and asked participants to recollect their feelings about their experiences in specific situations. Phenomenological studies focused their attention on the participants' recollection of their past experiences and used how the participants perceived they felt in a specific situation to generate data.

The intertwined, intricate details of the employees' situation that could provide additional insight into why the employee with CTS felt helpless were what was missing from these studies. Examples of the intertwined, intricate details might include the color of the room the employee was standing in when speaking to their co-worker, or the smell of the manager's cologne when he or she was being written up, or how the employees felt at that exact moment when they saw their name attached to that write-up. The intertwined details, Adler (2009), Alvarez, Pagani, & Meucci (2012), Keady and Jones (2010), and LeVine (2012) argued, are what provide additional insight into the employees with CTS' experience and understanding into their "individual reality" (Adler, 2009, p. 610). Once inside the employees with CTS' individual realities, Alvarez et al. (2012), Keady and Jones (2010), and LeVine (2012) argued that the details provide the exposition to learn how and why employees with CTS acted the way they did during situations. This assertion is consistent with the arguments of Lupien, Seery, and Almonte (2012) and Maas, Taal, Van der Linden, and Boonen (2009) and with constructivist ground theory literature (Charmaz, 2014; Glaser & Strauss, 1967/2009; Guba & Lincoln, 1989; Morse, 2010), which emphasizes the individuality brought to the study through the participants' own words. Furthermore, the BPS model emphasizes the importance of uncovering the psychological, physical, and sociological details of the participants' stories in order to learn the full meaning of employees with CTS' individual realities.

Physical Symptoms

Case studies generalized the employees' pain and their ability to do their jobs (Gelfman et al., 2009; Haanpää et al., 2009; Magee, 2014; van Rin, Huisstede, Koes, & Burdof, 2009). Phenomenological studies discussed employee pain ratio (Blau et al., 2013; O'Rourke, 2014; Owens & Van Ittersum, 2013) and provided statistics regarding their grip strength (Buhaug, Moen, & Irgens, 2014; House et al., 2014; Marks et al., 2011).

However, findings in this study showed that there is a large difference between saying in a case study, "Treatment and follow-up may lead to significant benefits in healthcare" (Alfonso, Jann, Mass, & Torreggiani, 2009, p. 243) or in a phenomenological study, "Data indicate a correlation of strength, range of motion, fulfillment of expectations, deformity, workers' compensation, and length of follow-up with satisfaction" (Marks et al., 2011)and an employee with CTS's saying in an open-ended interview, "The throbbing in my wrist got so bad that I had to wear my brace at night in order to sleep," Or as one employee with CTS stated in the semi-structured interview, "Things slide out of my hand because I cannot hold on to them. I've lost my ability to grip!" The latter statements show what it is like to have CTS on an everyday basis and physically depict what employees with CTS experience with this disease.

This distinction is consistent with constructivist grounded theory methodology, which states people use their experience to define and relate to their reality (Guba & Lincoln, 1989). Charmaz (2014) argued that data does not provide a window on reality. However, the employees with CTS who described not being able to hold objects in their hands related that inability to their perception that the effects of CTS have taken away their ability to do everyday things.

Mental Symptoms

Mental symptomology was not specifically addressed or discussed in case studies or phenomenological studies surrounding employees with CTS. The usage of the term *mental* in this constructivist grounded theory study referred to the psychological discomfort employees with CTS experienced during their workday, which were depicted in the subcategories of (a) loss of control, (b) fear regarding job stability, (c) emotional instability, and (d) social isolation. Each of these subcategories is discussed below.

Loss of control. Loss of control in case studies (Giersiepen & Spallek, 2011; Harris-Adamson et al., 2013; Nordander et al., 2009; Silverstein et al., 2010) and phenomenological studies (Ammann, Satink, & Andresen, 2012; Brattig, Schablon, Nienhaus, & Peters, 2014; Chalmer et al. 2012; Long, Burgess-Limerick, & Stapleton, 2014) was depicted through employees' recollections of how they lost control or why they lost control. However, in this study, the context of how employees with CTS lost control showed a direct correlation to the pattern of events that occurred. Findings in this study showed that employees with CTS who had a negative physical experience with their symptoms also had a negative mental experience. What this means is that employees whose negative physical experience with CTS crept into their mental state of being produced negative thoughts and consequences for them. This finding is consistent with the argument made by Heijbel et al. (2006) and the BPS model, that in order for an employees with CTS to be physically well, they have to be mentally well and vice-versa. The BPS model shows that a person's physical well-being has a direct correlation to their mental well-being, and if one of these are not in alignment with the other, then both will be affected.

Social isolation. Social isolation was found in both case studies and phenomenological studies, with a specific reference to bullying

(Einarsen et al., 2009; Rugulies, 2012; Sloan et al., 2010). However, like other case studies and phenomenological studies, they still lacked the small details about the employees with CTS' physical, mental, and social plight.

The BPS model shows a direct relationship between the physical, psychological, and sociological symptoms associated with employees' experience with an illness. This assertion was confirmed by several case and phenomenological studies surrounding bullying that targeted employees with CTS. Research showed that the implied, intended outcome of bullying was to eliminate the employees with CTS through physical and mental harassment (Devonish, 2013; Glasø et al., 2011), social exclusion (Appelbaum et al., 2012; Fevre et al., 2013), and "verbal abuse, accusations, and public humiliation" (Hauge et al., 2010, p. 427).

Employees with CTS in this study confirmed case study and phenomenological study statements with details of their stories. One employee with CTS stated that she was publicly humiliated when their manager read their status report out loud and corrected her grammar. The employee with CTS reported that this experience caused her to physically modify her behavior by spending hours writing her status reports, versus the minutes it used to take because she feared being publicly humiliated again. The physical change in effort showed the psychological and sociological impact this experience had for this employee with CTS because it indirectly caused her to physically modify her behavior. This finding is consistent with the BPS model and the arguments made by Silva et al. (2010), Silverstein et al. (2010), and De, Vranceanu, and Ring (2013), who stated that sociological and psychological stress and stressors can directly impact the physical temperament and coping strategy that an employees with CTS will implement into their lives in an attempt to align and alleviate their social and psychological stress.

Psychological Symptoms

Qualitative studies examining the psychological effects of CTS described the employees with CTS' experience of depression and anxiety, but did not discuss or reference self-induced isolation. Therefore, it can be assumed that this was a new psychological experience found within this study. Additionally, case studies and phenomenological studies described the employees with CTS' experience of having depression and anxiety, but researchers did not discuss the exposition behind how or why the employees with CTS experienced these psychological symptoms, how they manifested themselves within each other, and how they had the ability to intensify their effects when the employees with CTS experienced additional self-perceived psychological stress or trauma.

Because there was no previous literature found regarding self-induced isolation to make or draw a definition from, it is assumed that self-induced isolation is the process wherein people choose to remove themselves from physical contact from the population that caused the self-perceived psychological stress or trauma to occur.

Physical and Psychological Symptoms

Physical and psychological symptoms, along with their supporting subcategories, depression and anxiety and panic attacks, proved to be very important in influencing how employees with CTS viewed their illness because their physical symptom of CTS could trigger psychological reaction symptoms to occur within themselves and vice versa.

Phenomenological studies conducted by Egan et al. (2009), Franche et al. (2009), West et al. (2012), Wynne-Jones et al. (2011), and Westgaard and Winkel (2010) stated that the combined effects of physical and psychological symptoms caused employees with CTS continued loss of control over their situations and perpetuated the intensity of these effects over time when left untreated. This finding is consistent with the BPS model, which argues there is a "relationship between the individual and his environment, which through constructivism explains how an individual perceives his environment" (Adler, 2009, p. 607).

Depression and anxiety. Case studies and phenomenological studies emphasized that depression and anxiety occurred for employees with CTS because they experienced hierarchal bullying. Hierarchal bullying is an "abuse of power" (Schumann et al., 2014, p. 846) accomplished through psychological mind control, manipulation (D'Cruz & Noronha, 2010; De Cuyper et al., 2009; Einarsen et al., 2009; Einarsen et al., 2011; Finne et al., 2011; Schumann et al., 2014), and discrediting the employee with co-workers (Hoefsmit et al., 2013; Hogh et al., 2011; Idris et al., 2014; Law et al., 2011).

Employees with CTS in this study reported that it was the combination of the physical and psychological encounters with co-workers and employers that caused them to experience their physical and psychological symptoms as a coping mechanism within their environment. One employee with CTS stated in his or her open-ended interview,

> When my symptoms flared up, I stayed home because my boss wasn't at my house and able to give me grief over what I had not done the day before. My time at home meant I had peace. After a while, however, he caught on, and I was written up for my excessive absenteeism. I spent a lot of time in the bathroom and I got written up for that, too. After a while I just sat at my desk and felt myself bloat out and get sicker and sicker.

The employee with CTS's experience aligns with the BPS model by showing how the physical aspect of CTS directly impacted the psychological and sociological aspect of this disease. The employer's taking away the employee's psychological coping mechanism of staying home directly affected the employee's temperament and mental health, and forced the employee with CTS into social regression. The employee with CTS now had to attempt to mentally treat their physical symptoms by overcompensating with their sociological aspect (Appendix C). When the sociological coping mechanism was taken away, the employee with CTS was forced to deal with his or her symptoms, with no way of doing it (Appendix D).

Panic attacks. Case studies and phenomenological studies discussed panic attacks as a general psychological symptom for employees with CTS (Hauge et al., 2010; Idris et al., 2014; Shoss & Shoss, 2012; Vie, Glasø, & Einarsen, 2010). However, employees with CTS' statements of the walls "swirling around them" and of their "not being able to breathe" revealed the after effects of repeatedly being exposed to bullying from employers and co-workers. This is consistent with the methodology implied by the BPS model which states that the employees with CTS' panic attacks were their psychological coping mechanism that was induced by some form of trauma—physical, psychological, or social.

Loss of self-esteem and waiting for the inevitable. Case studies and phenomenological studies examining the sociological effects of

CTS did not discuss or reference loss of self-esteem or waiting for the inevitable specifically in their studies. Therefore, it is assumed that both were new sociological experiences found within this study. Their effects and rationale are discussed below.

Loss of self-esteem. Participants revealed when they experienced negative sociological interactions with their co-workers and employers that their psychological senses were heightened to their surroundings and their injury. This effect is consistent with the BPS model, which shows that self-esteem is directly affected by a person's psychological and physical sense of self. Further, current studies surrounding the effects of negative self-esteem show that the loss of self-esteem has serious stigmas associated with it, which have been shown to affect a person psychologically and sociologically. Link, Struening, Neese-Todd, Asmussen, and Phelan (2014) argued that loss of self-esteem produces psychological feelings of "failure" (p. 1,621) and loneliness (F. Kong & You, 2013), which can directly impact psychological and sociological "life satisfaction" (Lupien et al., 2012, p. 763), including "identity loss" (Kirsh et al., 2012, p. 145), and barriers to future employment opportunities (F. Kong & You, 2013). Additional studies are being conducted to determine if loss of self-esteem can contribute directly to people's developing and experiencing depression (Sowislo & Orth, 2013; Thoits, 2013).

Waiting for the inevitable. Employees with CTS reported having heightened psychological sensitivity to their surroundings and their injury because of the physical limitations that CTS caused in their workday. This phenomenon aligns with the BPS model, which shows that employees experienced a heightened psychological response to their surroundings as a coping skill brought on by comments from their co-workers and employers in their social environment.

This finding was confirmed in psychological and sociological studies, which argued that there is a direct link to "workplace wellness" (Jung & Cha, 2013, p. 443) and an employee's physical, psychological, and social well-being (Avey, Luthans, Smith, &Palmer, 2010; Jung & Cha, 2013; Page & Vella-Brodrick, 2009; Panaccio & Vandenberghe, 2009; Shier & Graham, 2011). Studies also emphasized the consequences of not having or maintaining consistent workplace wellness, which included excessive employee turnover (Kronstrom et al., 2011; Walker & Heffner, 2009), depressed employees (Hershcovis, 2011; Parzefall &

Salin, 2010), and excessive absenteeism (Jung & Cha, 2013; Kirsh et al., 2012; Panaccio & Vandenberghe, 2009).

Limitations

The original premise behind this study was to discover how the physical, social, and emotional effects of carpal tunnel syndrome (CTS) affected employees' ability to complete an employer-sponsored Return to Work (RTW) program at their place of employment. Through a constructivist grounded theory approach using semi-structured interviews, body language observations, and open-ended interviews, relationships between employees, their managers, and their co-workers were examined.

The results found in this study were consistent with current case studies and phenomenological studies that measured the effects of CTS, along with several sociological studies that measured the new sociological experiences found within this study. However, while there were several strengths found with this study in terms of the methodology and theory, there were also limitations, which are discussed below. Three limitations present in this study were (a) study had a small sample size; (b) the research limited only to employees with CTS; and (c) the researcher was solely responsible for collecting and analyzing the data in this study.

Sample Size

The sample size for this study was 12 participants, five men and seven women, which created limited theories because data saturation was reached after six open-ended interviews. Thus, it could be argued if the sample study size were larger, then additional theories could have been generated from additional data. The additional experiences could have also provided additional insight into answering the research questions.

Limitations in Scope and Focus

This study was originally designed to learn and measure how the effects of CTS prohibited employees with CTS from completing their employers' RTW programs by interviewing the employees with CTS, their managers, and their co-workers. However, IRB approval was not granted for the original design because the researcher was told that (a) the study would be too large in focus, (b) too difficult to complete in a six-month time frame; (c) too risky because the chance of employers' seeking retaliation against the employees with CTS or their co-workers for participating would jeopardize the integrity and credibility of the study. The study was redesigned to include only the employees with CTS and their experience. Therefore, it can be argued if employers' and co-workers' experiences could have been accounted for in this study, additional insight and theories could have been generated and used to answer the research questions. Additionally, because the study was redesigned, one of the research questions, which was specific to the employers' feelings about RTW programs and employees with CTS, was eliminated. Findings from this question could have also been used to generate additional theories and answer the research questions.

Risk of Possibility of Researcher Bias

I was solely responsible for interviewing, collecting, and analyzing the research data in this study. Because I have previous, personal experience with CTS in the workplace, it could be inferred that my personal experience with CTS could have clouded judgment or steered the creation of the open-ended research questions. To reduce bias in this study, I concentrated study efforts on aspects of the disease that I had not personally known or experienced. I also utilized Strauss and Corbin's (1998) "seven point criterion checklist" (Kenealy, 2008, para. 22) in conjunction with semi-structured interviews, observations, and field notes to create individualized open-ended interview questions that were unique to the individual employee's psychological, psychosomatic, and social experience with CTS in the workplace.

Recommendations for Further Research

Considering the challenges expressed by employees with CTS in this study and the new sociological findings that emerged, additional grounded theory studies are recommended to examine how the effects of CTS financially extend to the employer and co-workers of employees with CTS. The purpose of this study would be to confirm previous claims made in other studies about reducing workers' compensation claim insurance cost.

Additional studies examining the physical, psychological, psychosomatic, and sociological realms CTS has for employers with employees who have CTS and their co-workers are also recommended to examine how this disease affects them in and out of the workplace. Because of the risk of retaliation against employees with CTS, research with different employers and co-workers from separate organizations is recommended. A larger sample size and multiple organizations are also recommended to adequately measure this.

Conclusion

The purpose of this study was to measure the effects of carpal tunnel syndrome (CTS) in the workplace. Through semi-structured interviews, open-ended interviews, and observations conducted during these interviews, stories and theories emerged through the employees with CTS' intimate details and provided missing insight into the their experience in the workplace. Theories that emerged were the result of using (a) open coding to show the Kantianisms of this disease, (b) axial coding to put the data separated during open coding back together, and (c) selective coding, which revealed an insider's perspective on how CTS affected employees with CTS on psychological, psychosomatic, and sociological levels both in and out of the RTW program and within their personal lives.

Findings in this study revealed that there were direct bi- and tri-directional cause and effect relationships between the physical symptoms employees with CTS experienced and the psychological and psychosomatic effects that indirectly caused the reported physical symptoms to occur, re-occur, and progressively get worse. This finding was confirmed and validated through the biopsychosocial (BPS) model, which provided the additional sociological explanatory framework into the employees with CTS' "individual realities]" (Adler, 2009, p. 610).

The concepts and theories that emerged from this study are important because the employees with CTS' own personal accounts and experiences with this disease in and out of the workplace derived them. It is my hope that the findings from this study be used to create RTW programs that effectively manage the physical, psychological, psychosomatic, and sociological Kantianisms and crucibles of this disease.

REFERENCES

Abasolo, L., Lajas, C., Leon, L., Carmona, L., & Macarron, P. (2012). Prognostic factors for long-term work disability due to musculoskeletal disorders. *Rheumatology International, 32,* 3,831-3,839. doi:10.1007/s00296-011-2264-5

Adler, R. H. (2009). Engel's biopsychosocial model is still relevant today. *Journal of Psychosomatic Research, 67,* 607-611. doi:10.1016/j.jpsychores.2009.08.008

AFA Insurance. (2009). Serious work accidents and long-term sick leave. Stockholm, Sweden: Author.

Agervold, M. (2009). The significance of organizational factors for the incidence of bullying. *Scandinavian Journal of Psychology. 50,* 267-276. doi:10.1111/j.1467-9450.2009.00710.x

Ahlstrom, F., Hagberg, M., & Dellve, L. (2013). Workplace rehabilitation and supportive conditions at work: A prospective study. *Journal of Occupational Rehabilitation, 23,* 248-260. doi:10.1007/s10926-012-9391-z

Alfonso, C., Jann, S., Massa, R., & Torreggiani, A. (2010). Diagnosis, treatment and follow-up of the carpal tunnel syndrome: A review. *Neurological Sciences, 31*(3), 243-252. doi:10.1007/s10072-009-0213-9

Alvarez, A. S., Pagani, M., & Meucci, P. (2012). The clinical application of the biopscyhosocial model in mental health. *American Journal of Physical Medicince & Rehabilitaiton.* 91(13), 173-180. doi:10.1097/phm.0b013e31823d54be

Ammann, B., Satink, T., & Andresen, M. (2012). Experiencing occupations with chronic hand disability: Narratives of hand-injured adults. *Hand Therapy, 17*(4), 87-94. doi:10.1177/1758998312471253

Ammendolia, C., Cassidy, D., Steenstra, I., Soklaridis, S., Boyle, E., Eng., S., . . . Côté., P. (2009). Designing a workplace return-to-work program for occupational low back pain: an intervention mapping approach. *BMC Musculoskeletal Disorders, 10.* doi:10.1186/1471-2474-10-65

Anderson, M., F., Nielsen, K., M., & Brinkmann, S. (2012). Meta-synthesis of qualitative research on return to work among employees with common mental disorders. *Scandinavian Journal of Work, Environment & Health. 38,* 93-104. doi:10.5271/sjweh.3257

Appelbaum, S. H., Semerjian, G., & Mohan, K. (2012). Workplace bullying: Consequences, causes and controls (Part 1). *Industrial and Commercial Training, 44,* 203-210. doi:10.1108/00197851211231478

Armstrong, P. (2011). Budgetary bullying. *Critical Perspectives on Accounting, 22,* 632-643. doi:10.1016/j.cpa.2011.01.011

Atkinson, C. (2014). Bullying and harassment. *Occupational Health, 66,* 22-24.

Atroshi, I., Lyren, P. E., & Gummesson, C. (2009). The 6-Item CTS Symptoms Scale: A brief outcomes measure for carpal tunnel syndrome. *Quality Life Research, 18,* 347-358. doi:10.1007/s11136-009-9449-3

Avey, J. B., Luthans, F., Smith, R. M., & Palmer, N. F. (2010). Impact of positive psychological capital on employee well-being over time. *Journal of Occupational Health Psychology, 15*(1), 17-23. doi:10.1037/a0016998

Baillien, E., De Cuyper, N., & De Witte, H. (2011). Job autonomy and workload as antecedents of workplace bullying: A two-wave test of Karasek's Job Demand Control Model for targets and perpetrators. *Journal of Occupational and Organizational Psychology, 84,* 191–208. doi:10.1348/096317910x508371

Baldwin, M. L., & Butler, R. J. (2006). Upper extremity disorders in the workplace: Costs and outcomes beyond the first return to work. *Journal of Occupational Rehabilitation, 16,* 303-323. doi:10.1007/s10926-006-9043-2

Banerjee, U., Bhattacharya, N. K., & Sanyal, N. (2014). Stress, coping and emotional processing in chronic pain: A comparative analysis. *SIS Journal of Projective Psychology & Mental Health, 21,* 104-112.

Banham, R. (1994). The new risk in ergonomic solutions. *Risk Management, 41,* 22-30.

Bartlett, J. E., & Bartlett, M. E. (2011). Workplace bullying: An integrative literature review. *Advances in Developing Human Resources, 13,* 69-84. doi:10.1177/1523422311410651

Beirne, M., & Hunter, P. (2013). Workplace bullying and the challenge of pre-emptive management. *Personnel Review, 42,* 595-612. doi:10.1108/PR-07-2012-0105

Berger, M., Vermeulen, M., Koelman, J. H. T. M., van Schaik, I. N., & Roos, Y. B. W. E. M. (2012). The long-term follow-up of treatment with corticosteroid injections in patients with carpal tunnel syndrome. When are multiple injections indicated? *Journal of Hand Surgery Europe, 38,* 634-639. doi:10.1177/1753193412469580

Berthelsen, M., Skogstad, A., Lau, B, & Einarsen, S. (2011). Do they stay or do they go? *International Journal of Manpower, 32(2),* 178-193. doi:10.1108/01437721111130198

Blau, G., Monos, C., Boyer, K. D., Davis, K., Flanagan, R., Lopez, A., & Tatum, D. S. (2013). Correlates of injury-forced work reduction for massage therapists and bodywork practitioners. *International Journal of Therapeutic Massage & Bodywork, 6(3),* 6-18. doi:10.3822/ijtmb.v6i3.199

Board, B. J., & Brown, J. (2010). Barriers and enablers to returning to work from long-term sickness absence: Part 1 – A quantitative perspective. *American Journal of Industrial Medicine, 54,* 307-324. doi:10.1002/AJIM.20889

Boddy, C. R. (2011). Corporate psychopaths, bullying and unfair supervision in the workplace. *Journal of Business Ethics, 100,* 367-379. doi:10.1007/s10551-010-0689-5

Boundless. (2014). The biopsychosocial model. Retrieved from https://www.boundless.com/psychology/textbooks/boundless-psychology-textbook/stress-and-health-psychology-17/models-for-positive-change-86/the-biopsychosocial-model-326-12861/

Brattig, B., Schablon, A., Nienhaus, A., & Peters, C. (2014). Occupational accident and disease claims, work-related stress and job satisfaction of physiotherapists. *Journal of Occupational Medicine and Toxicology, 9*(1), 36-49. doi:10.1186/s12995-014-0036-3

Brotheridge, C. M., & Lee, R. T. (2010). Restless and confused: Emotional responses to workplace bullying in men and women. *Career Development International, 15,* 687–707. doi:10.1108/13620431011094087

Brouwer, S., Krol, B., Reneman, M. F., Bultmann, U., Franceh, R. L., van der Klink, J. L. J., & Groothoff, J. W. (2009). Behavioral determinants as predictors of return to work after long-term sickness absence: An application of the theory of planned behavior. *Journal of Occupational Rehabilitation, 19,* 166-174. doi:10.1007/s10926-009-9172-5

Buhaug, K., Moen, B. E., & Irgens, Å. (2014). Upper limb disability in Norwegian workers with hand-arm vibration syndrome. *Journal of Occupational Medicine and Toxicology, 9*(1), 5. doi:10.1186/1745-6673-9-5

Butler, G. (2002). Getting the tough cases back to work. *Risk Management, 49,* 1-4.

Cano, A., Leong, L. L., Heller, J. B., & Lutz, J. R. (2009). Perceived entitlement to pain-related support and pain catastrophizing: Associations with perceived and observed support. *Pain, 147,* 249-254. doi:10.1016/j.pain.2009.09.023

Carbo, J., & Hughes, A. (2010). Workplace bullying: Developing a human rights definition from the perspective and experiences of targets. *Working USA, 13,* 387-403. doi:10.1111/j.1743-4580.2010.00297.x

Carroll, C., Rick, J., Pilgrim, H., Cameron, J., & Hillage, J. (2010). Workplace involvement improves return to work rates among employees with back pain on long-term sick leave: A systematic review of the effectiveness and cost-effectiveness of interventions. *Disability & Rehabilitation, 32,* 607-621. doi:10.3109/09638280903186301

Centineo, J. (1986). Return to work programs: Cut costs and employee turnover. *Risk Management, 33,* 44. Retrieved from http://www.rims.org/Pages/Default.aspx

Chalmer, J., Blakeway, M., Adams, Z., Milan, S., Donnan, M., Jerosch-Herold, C., . . . Juzl, E. (2012). Scientific and clinical paper abstracts from the British Association of Hand Therapists

Annual Conference 2012. *Hand Therapy,* *17*(4). 100-103. doi:10.1258/ht.2012.012014

Charmaz, K. (2014). *Constructing grounded theory.* Los Angeles, CA: Sage.

Cho, S., Zunin, I. D., Chao, P. J., Heiby, E. M., & Mckoy, J. (2012). Effects of pain controllability and discrepancy in social support on depressed mood among patients with chronic pain. *International Journal of Behavioral Medicine, 19,* 270-279. doi: 10.1007/s12529-011-9175-4

Congressional Review Act, Pub. L. No. 104-121, 104th Cong., Stat. 847 (1996).

Clay, C., & Olitt, R. (2012). *Peer power: Transforming workplace relationships.* New York, NY: John Wiley & Sons.

Corbin, J., & Strauss, A. (2008). *Basics of qualitative research* (3rd ed.). Los Angeles, CA: Sage.

Cornelius, L., R., van der Klink, J., J., Groothoff, J., W., Brouwer, S. (2011). Prognostic factors of long-term disability due to mental disorders: A systematic review. *Journal of Occupational and Rehabilitation, 21,* 259–274. doi:10.1007/s10926-010-9261-5

Côté, D., & Coutu, F.-M. (2010). A critical review of gender issues in understanding prolonged disability related to musculoskeletal pain: How are they relevant to rehabilitation? *Disability and Rehabilitation, 32,* 87-102. doi:10.3109/09638280903026572

Creswell, J. W. (2009). *Research design.* Los Angeles, CA: Sage.

Creswell, J. W. (2012). *Qualitative inquiry and research design.* Los Angeles, CA: Sage.

Crotty, M. (1998). *The foundations of social research.* Los Angeles, CA: Sage.

Dae-seok, K., Gold, J., & Kim, D. (2012). Responses to job insecurity. *Career Development International, 17*(4), 314-322. doi:10.1108/13620431211255815

Dale, L., Barkley, A., Bayless, S., Coleman, S. D., McDonald, B., Myszkowski, J., & Phipps-Stevens, L. (2003). Experience of cumulative trauma disorders on life roles of workers and family members: A case study of a married couple. *Work, 20,* 245-255. Retrieved from PubMed.gov. (PMID: 12775930)

Davidson, D., & Harrington, K. V. (2012). Workplace bullying: It's not just about lunch money any more. *Southern Journal of Business & Ethics, 4,* 493-99.

D'Cruz, P., & Noronha, E. (2010). The exit coping response to workplace bullying. *Employee Relations, 32,* 102-120. doi:10.1108/01425451011010078

De Cuyper, N., Baillien, E., & De Witte, H.. (2009). Job insecurity, perceived employability and targets' and perpetrators' experiences of workplace bullying. *Work & Stress, 23,* 206-224. doi:10.1080/02678370903257578

De, S. D., Vranceanu, A. M., & Ring, D. C. (2013). Contribution of kinesophobia and catastrophic thinking to upper-extremity-specific disability. *The Journal of Bone & Joint Surgery, 95*(1), 76-81doi:10.2106/jbjs.l.00064

De Souza, L., & Frank, A. O. (2011). Patients' experiences of the impact of chronic back pain on family life and work. *Disability and Rehabilitation Journal, 33,* 310-318. doi:10.3109/09638288.2 010.490865

Devonish, D. (2013). Workplace bullying, employee performance and behaviors: The mediating role of psychological well-being. *Employee Relations, 35,* 630-647. doi:10.1108/ER-01-2013-0004

DiCicco-Bloom, B., & Crabtree, F. B. (2006). The qualitative research interview. *Medical Education, 40,* 314-321. doi: 10.1111/j.1365-2929.2006.02418.x

Dillenberger, C. (2009). Six steps to a successful Return to Work program. *Business Management Report.* Retrieved from www. ioma.com

Doll, B., Strein, W., Jacob, S., & Prasse, D. P. (2011). Youth privacy when educational records include ssychological records. *Professional Psychology: Research and Practice, 42,* 259-268. doi:10.1037/ a0023685

Dow, C. M., Roche, P. A., & Ziebland, S. (2012). Talk of frustration in the narratives of people with chronic pain. *Chronic Illness, 8,* 176-193. doi:10.1177/1742395312443692

Druss, B. G., Hwang, I., Petukhova, M., Sampson, N. A., & Kessler, R. C. (2009). Impairment in role functioning in mental and chronic medical disorders in the United States: Results from the

National Comorbidity Survey Replication. *Molecular Psychiatry,*
14, 728-737. doi:10.1038/mp.2008.13

Drutman, L. (2004). Repetitively straining workers. *Multinational*
Monitor, 25, 17-18.

Dunstan, D. A., & MacEachen, E. (2013). Bearing the brunt: Co-
workers' experiences of work reintegration processes. *Journal*
of Occupational Rehabilitation, 23, 44-54. doi:10.1007/
s10926-012-9380-2

Eakin, J., M. (2010). Towards a "standpoint" perspective: Health
and safety in small workplaces from the perspective of the
workers. *Institution of Occupational Safety and Health. 2,*
113-127. Retrieved from http://www.academia.edu/1546192/
Towards_a_standpoint_perspective_Occupational_health_and_safety_
from_the_perspective_of_the_workers

Egan, M., Bambra, C., Petticrew, M., & Whitehead, M. (2009).
Reviewing evidence on complex social interventions: Appraising
implementation in systematic reviews of the health effects
of organizational-level workplace interventions. *Journal of*
Epidemiology Community Health, 63, 4-11. doi:10.1136/
jech.2007.071233

Einarsen, S., Hoel, H., & Notelaers, G. (2009). Measuring bullying and
harassment at work: Validity, factor structure, and psychometric
properties of the Negative Acts Questionnaire Revised. *Work &*
Stress, 23, 24-44. doi:10.1080/02678370902815673

Einarsen, S., Hoel, H., Zapf, D., & Cooper, C. L. (2011). *Bullying and*
harassment in the workplace. Boca Raton, FL: Taylor & Francis
Group.

Emotional. (2013). *Dictionary.com.* Retrieved from http://dictionary.
reference.com/browse/emotional?s=t

Essex, N. L. (2009). *The 200 most frequently asked legal questions for*
educators. Thousand Oaks, CA: Corwin.

Evanoff, B., & Kymes, S. (2010). Modeling the cost benefit of nerve
conduction studies in pre-employment screening for Carpal
Tunnel Syndrome. *Scandinavian Journal of Work, Environment*
& Health, 36, 299-304. doi:10.5271/sjwch.3030

Faucett, J., Blanc, P. D., & Yelin, E. (2000). The impact of carpal tunnel
syndrome on work status: Implications of job characteristics for

staying on the job. *Journal of Occupational Rehabilitation, 10,* 55-69. doi:10.1023/a:1009441828933

Fevre, R., Robinson, A., Lewis, D., & Jones, T. (2013). The ill-treatment of employees with disabilities in British workplaces. *Work, Employment and Society, 27,* 288-307. doi:10.1177/0950017012460311

Finne, L. B., Knardahl, S., & Lau, B. (2011), Workplace bullying and mental distress: A prospective study of Norwegian employees. *Scandinavian Journal Work Environmental Health, 37,* 276-287. doi:10.5271/sjweh.3156

Franche, R.-L., Carndie, N., Johnson, S. H., Côté, P., Breslin, F. C., Bultmann, U., . . . Krause, N., (2009). Course, diagnosis, and treatment of depressive symptomatology in workers following a workplace injury: A prospective cohort study. *Canadian Journal of Psychiatry, 54,* 534-546.

Franche, R.-L., Corbiere, M., Lee, H., Breslin, F. C., & Hepburn, C. G. (2007). The readiness for Return-To-Work (RRTW) scale: Development and validation of a self-report staging scale in lost-time claimants with musculoskeletal disorders. *Journal of Occupational Rehabilitation, 17,* 450-472.

Gauthier, N., Thibault, P., & Sullivan, M. J. L. (2011). Catastrophizers with chronic pain display more pain behavior when in a relationship with a low catastrophizing spouse. *Pain Research & Management, 16,* 293-299. Retrieved from PubMed.gov. (PMID: 22059198)

Gelfman, R., Melton, L. J., Yawn, B. P., Wollan, P. C., Amadio, P. C., & Stevens, J. C. (2009). Long-term trends in carpal tunnel syndrome. *Neurology, 72*(1), 33-41. doi:10.1212/01. wnl.0000338533.88960.b9

Georgakopoulos, A., Wilkin, L., & Kent, B. (2011). Workplace bullying: A complex problem in contemporary organizations. *International Journal of Business and Social Science.* 2, 1-20. Retrieved from http://ijbssnet.com/journals/ Vol._2_No._3_%5BSpecial_Issue_-_January_2011%5D/1.pdf

Ghasemi, M., Rezaee, M., Chavoshi, F., Mojtahed, M., & Koushki, E. S. (2012). Carpal tunnel syndrome: The role of occupational factors among 906 workers. *Trauma Monthly, 17,* 296-300. doi:10.5812/traumamon.6554

Ghezeljeh, T. N., & Emami, A. (2009). Grounded theory: Methodology and philosophical perspective. *Nurse Researcher, 17,* 15-23. Retrieved from PubMed.gov. (PMID: 19911650)

Gholipour, A., Sanjari, S. S., Bod, M., & Kozekanan, S. F. (2011). Organizational bullying and women stress in workplace. *International Journal of Business Management, 6,* 234-241. doi:10.5539/ijbm.v6n6p234

Giersiepen, K., & Spallek, M. (2011). Carpal tunnel syndrome as an occupational disease. *Deutsches Ärzteblatt International, 108*(14), 238-242. doi:10.3238%2Farztebl.2011.0238

Gilbreath, B. (2012). Educating mangers to create healthy workplaces. *Journal of Management Education, 36,* 166-190. doi:10.1177/1052562911430206

Glaser, B. G., & Strauss, A. L. (2009). *The discovery of grounded theory: Strategies for qualitative research.* New Brunswick, NJ: Transaction Publishers. Originally published 1967.

Glaso, L., Nielsen, M. B., Einarsen S., Haugland K., & Matthiesen, S. B. (2009a). Basic assumptions and post-traumatic stress disease among targets of workplace bullying. *Journal of Norwegian Psychological Association. 46,* 153–160.

Glaso, L., Nielsen, M. B., Einarsen S., Haugland K., & Matthiesen, S. B. (2009b). Interpersonal problems among perpetrators and targets of workplace bullying. *Journal of Applied Psychology, 39,* 1,316-1,333.

Glaso, L., Vie, T. L., Holmdal, G. R., & Einarsen, S. (2011). An application of affective events theory to workplace bullying: The role of emotions, trait anxiety, and trait anger. *European Psychologist, 16,* 198-208. doi:10.1027/1016-9040/a000026

Gravel, S., Vissandjee, B., Lippel, K., Broudeur, J.-M., Patry, L., & Champagne, F. (2010). Ethics and the compensation of immigrant workers for work-related injuries and illnesses. *Journal of Immigrant Minority Health. 12,* 707-714. doi:10.1007/s10903-008-9208-5

Groenwald, T. (2004). A phenomenological research design illustrated. *International Journal of Qualitative Methods, 3,* 1-26.

Guba, E., & Lincoln, Y. (1989). *Fourth generation evaluation.* Newbury Park, CA: Sage.

Guba, E., & Lincoln, Y. (2001). Guidelines and checklist for constructivist (a.k.a fourth generation) evaluation. Retrieved from http://www. wmich.edu/evalctr/archive_checklists/constructivisteval.pdf

Gumbus, A., & Lyons, B. (2011). Workplace harassment: The social costs of bullying. *Journal of Leadership, Accountability and Ethics*, *8*, 72-90. Retrieved from http://digitalcommons.sacredheart. edu/cgi/viewcontent.cgi?article=1106&context=wcob_fac

Gumbus, A., & Meglich, P. (2012). Lean and mean: Workplace culture and the prevention of workplace bullying. *The Journal of Applied Business and Economics. 13*, 11-20. Retrieved from http://digitalcommons.sacredheart.edu/cgi/viewcontent.cgi? article=1026&context=wcob_fac

Haanpää, M. L., Backonja, M. M., Bennett, M. I., Bouhassira, D., Cruccu, G., Hansson, P. T., . . . Baron, R. (2009). Assessment of neuropathic pain in primary care. *The American Journal of Medicine, 122*(10), 13-21. doi:10.1016/j.amjmed.2009.04.006

Hamilton, A. B. (2011). What is grounded theory, anyway? An overview with examples from qualitative research on women veterans. Retrieved from http://www.hsrd.research.va.gov/ for_researchers/cyber_seminars/archives/885-notes.pdf

Hammond, A., & Harriss, A. (2012). Impact of carpal tunnel syndrome. *Occupational Health, 64,* 14-16.

Harris-Adamson, C., Eisen, E. A., Dale, A. M., Evanoff, B., Hegmann, K. T., Thiese, M. S., . . . Rempel, D. (2013). Personal and workplace psychosocial risk factors for carpal tunnel syndrome: A pooled study cohort. *Occupational and Environmental Medicine, 70*(8), 529-537. doi:10.1136/oemed-2013-101365

Hasselberg, K., Jonsdottir, I. H., Ellbin, S., & Skagert, K. (2014). Self-reported stressors among patients with exhaustion disorder: An exploratory study of patient records. *BMC Psychiatry. 14*, 1-10. doi:10.1186/1471-244X-14-66

Hauge, L. J., Skogstad, A., & Einarsen, S. (2010). The relative impact of workplace bullying as a social stressor at work. *Scandinavian Journal of Psychology. 51*, 426-433. doi:10.1111/j.1467-9450.2010.00813.x

He, Y., Hu, J., Yu, I. T. S., Gu, W., & Liang, Y. (2010). Determinants of return to work after occupational injury. *Journal of Occupational Rehabilitation, 20*, 378-386. doi:10.1007/s:10926-010-9232-x

Heijbel, B., Josephson, M., Jensen, I., Stark, S., & Vingard, E. (2006). Return to work expectation predicts work in chronic musculoskeletal and behavioral health disorders: Prospective study with clinical implications. *Journal of Occupational Rehabilitation, 16*, 169-180. doi: 10.1007/s10926-006-9016-5

Hepburn, G., C., Franche, R.-L., & Francis, L. (2010). Successful return to work: The role of fairness and workplace based strategies. *International Journal of Workplace Health Management. 3*, 7-24. doi:10.1108/17538351011031902

Hershcovis, M. S. (2011). "Incivility, social undermining, bullying...oh my!": A call to reconcile constructs within workplace aggression research. *Journal of Organizational Behavior, 32*(3), 499-519. doi:10.1002/job.689

Hinduja, S. (2009). Occupational stressors and antinormative behavior. *Security Journal. 22*, 269-285. doi:10.1057/palgrave.sj.8350083

Hoefsmit, N., de Rijk, A., & Houkes, I. (2013). Work resumption at the price of distrust: A qualitative study on return to work legislation in the Netherlands. *BMC Public Health. 13*, 153-167. doi:10.1186/1471-2458-13-153

Hogh, A., Hoel, H., & Carneiro, I. G. (2011) Bullying and employee turnover among healthcare workers: A three-wave prospective study. *Journal of Nursing Management, 19*, 742–751. doi:10.1111/j.1365-2834.2011.01264.x

Hollins Martin, C. J., & Martin, C. (2010). Bully for you: harassment and bullying in the workplace. *British Journal of Midwifery, 18*(1), 25-31. doi:10.12968/bjom.2010.18.1.45812

Holmgren, K., & Ivanoff, S. D. (2007). Supervisors' views on employer responsibility in the return to work process: A focus group study. *Journal of Occupational Rehabilitation, 17,* 93-106. doi:10.1007/s10926-006-9041-4

House, R., Wills, M., Liss, G., Switzer-McIntyre, S., Lander, L., & Jiang, D. (2014). The effect of hand–arm vibration syndrome on quality of life. *Occupational Medicine, 64*(2), 133-135. doi:10.1093/occmed/kqt167

Houshmand, M., O'Reilly, J., Robinson, S., & Wolff, A. (2012). Escaping bullying: The simultaneous impact of individual and unit-level bullying on turnover intentions. *Human Relations, 65*, 901-918. doi:10.1177/0018726712445100

Huijs, J. J. J. M., Koppes, L. L. J., Taris, T. W., & Blonk, R. W. B. (2012). Differences in predictors of return to work among long-term sick-listed employees with different self-reported reasons for sick leave. *Journal of Occupational Rehabilitation, 22*, 301–11. doi:10.1007/s10926-011-9351-zHuman Factors and Ergonomics Society. (2010). About HFES. Retrieved from https://www.hfes.org/

Hunt, H. A. (2009). *The evolution of disability management in North American workers' compensation programs*. Victoria, British Columbia, Canada: W. E. UpJohn Institute for Employment Research. Retrieved from http://research.upjohn.org/reports/179

Idris, M. A., Dollard, M. F., & Yulita. (2014). Psychosocial safety climate, emotional demands, burnout, and depression: A longitudinal multilevel study in the Malaysian private sector. *Journal Of Occupational Health Psychology, 19*, 291-302. doi:10.1037/a0036599

Iles, R. A., Wyatt, M., & Pransky, G. (2012). Multi-faceted case management: Reducing compensation costs of musculoskeletal work injuries in Australia. *Journal of Occupational Rehabilitation, 22,* 478-488. doi:10.1007/s10926-012-9364-2

International Ergonomics Association. (2015). What is ergonomics: Definition and domains of ergonomics. Retrieved from http://www.iea.cc/whats/index.html

Jacobsen, H. B., Bjørngaard, J. H., Hara, K. W., Borchgrevink, P. C., Woodhouse, A., Landrø, N. I., . . . Stiles, T. C. (2014). The role of stress in absenteeism: Cortisol responsiveness among patients on long-term sick leave. *PLoS One*. 9, 1-9. doi:10.1371/journal.pone.0096048

Jenkins, P. J., Watts, A. C., Duckworth, A. D., & McEachan, J. E. (2012). Socioeconomic deprivation and the epidemiology of carpal tunnel syndrome. *Journal of Hand Surgery, 37*, 123-129. doi:10.1177/1753193411419952

Jerosch-Herold, C. J., Shepstone, L., Wilson, E. C. F., Dyer, T., & Blake, J. (2014). Clinical course, costs and predictive factors for response to treatment carpal tunnel syndrome: the PALMS study protocol. *BMC Musculoskeletal Disorders, 15,* 35. doi:10.1186/1471-2474-15-35

Julnes, G., & Bustelo, M. (2014). Professional values and ethics in evaluation. *American Journal of Evaluation, 35*(4). 525-526. doi:10.1177/1098214014549069

Jung, S. H., & Cha, Y. (2013). Wellness in the workplace: Health promotion programs. *Journal of Convergence Information Technology, 8*(13), 440-446. Retrieved from http://www.aicit.org/JCIT/ppl/JCIT3998PPL.pdf

Kantianism. (2015). Retrieved from Collins Dictionaries: http://www.collinsdictionary.com/dictionary/english/kantian

Keady, J., & Jones, L. (2010). Investigating the causes of behaviors that challenge in people with dementia. *Nursing Older People, 22*(9). 25-29. doi:10.7748/nop2010.11.22.9.25.c8061

Kenealy, G. (2008). Management research and grounded theory: A review of grounded theory building approach in organizational and management research. *The Grounded Theory Review, 7*(2), 95-117. Retrieved from http://groundedtheoryreview.com/2008/06/28/1004/

King, W., Tang., D., Luo, X., Sun Yu, I.T., Liang, Y., and He, Y. (2012) Prediction of Return To Work Outcomes Under an Injured Worker Case Management Program. *Journal of Occupational Rehabilitation. 22,* 230-240. DOI: 10.1007/s10926-011-9343-z

Kirsh, B., Slack, T., & King, C. A. (2012). The nature and impact of stigma towards injured workers. *Journal of Occupational Rehabilitation, 22,* 143-154. doi:10.1007/s10926-011-9335-z

Knauf, M. T., Schultz, I. Z., Stewart, A. M., & Gatchel, R. J. (2014). Models of Return to Work for musculoskeletal disorders: Advances in conceptualization and research. *Work and Disability. 431-452.* doi:10.1007/978-1-4939-0612-3_24

Koh, S. M., Moate, F., & Grinsell, D. (2009). Co-existing carpal tunnel syndrome in complex regional pain syndrome after hand trauma. *Journal of Hand Surgery Europe. 35,* 228-231. doi:10.1177/1753193409354015

Kong, F., & You, X. (2013). Loneliness and self-esteem as mediators between social support and life satisfaction in late adolescence. *Social Indicators Research, 110*(1), 271-279. doi:10.1007/s11205-011-9930-6

Kong, W., Tang, D., Xiaoyuan, L., Yu, I. T. S., Liang, Y., & He, Y. (2012). Prediction of return to work outcomes under an injured worker case management program. *Journal of Occupational Rehabilitation, 22,* 230-240.doi:10.1007/S10926-011-9343-Z

Kosny, A., Lifshen, M., Pugliese, D., Majesky, G., Kramer, D., Steenstra, I., . . . Carrasco, C. (2013). Buddies in bad times? The role of co-workers after a work-related injury. *Journal of Occupational Rehabilitation, 23,* 438-449. doi:10.1007/s10926-012-9411-z

Koukoulaki, T. (2010). New trends in work environment: New effects on safety. *Safety Science, 48,* 936-942. doi:10.1016/j.ssci.2009.04.003

Koukoulaki, T. (2013). The impact of lean production on musculoskeletal and psychosocial risks: An examination of sociotechnical trends over 20 years. *Hellenic Institute for Occupational Health & Safety, 45,* 198-212. doi:10.1016/j.apergo.2013.07.018

Kronstrom, K., Karlsson, H., Nabi, H., Oksanen, T., Salo, P., Sjosten, N., . . . Vahtera, J. (2011). Optimism and pessimism as predictors of work disability with a diagnosis of depression: A prospective cohort study of onset and recovery. *Journal of Affective Disorders, 130,* 294-299.

Lallukka, T., Haaramo, P., Rahkoenen, O., Sivertsen, B. (2013). Joint associations of sleep duration and insomnia symptoms with subsequent sickness absence: The Helsinki Health Study. *Scandinavian Journal Of Public Health, 41,* 516-523. doi:10.1177/1403494813481647

Lavie-Ajayi, M., Almog, N., & Krumer-Nevo, M. (2012). Chronic pain as a narratological distress: A phenomenological study. *Chronic Illness, 8,* 192-202. doi:10.1177/1742395312449665

Law, R., Dollard, M. F., Tuckey, M. R., & Dormann, C. (2011). Psychosocial safety climate as a lead indicator of workplace bullying and harassment, job resources, psychological health and employee engagement. *Accident Analysis & Prevention, 43,* 1,782-1,793. doi:10.1016/j.aap.2011.04.010

Letzring, T. D., & Snow, M. S. (2011). Mental health practitioners and HIPAA. *International Journal of Play Therapy, 20,* 153-164. doi: 10.1037/a0023717

LeVine, E. S. (2012). Facilitating recovery for people with serious mental illness employing a psychobiosocial model of care. *Professional Psychology: Research and Practice, 43*(1), 58-63. doi:10.1037/a0026889

Levy, D. (2006). Qualitative methodology and grounded theory in property research. *Pacific Rim Property Research Journal, 12*(4), 369-388. doi:10.1080/14445921.2006.11104216

Lewis, C., Mauffrey, C., Newman, S., Lambert, A., & Hull, P. (2009). Current concepts in carpal tunnel syndrome: A review of the literature. *European Journal Orthopedic Surgery & Traumatology, 20*, 445-452. doi:10.1007/s00590-010-0585-9

Link, B. G., Struening, E. L., Neese-Todd, S., Asmussen, S., & Phelan, J. C. (2014). Stigma as a barrier to recovery: The consequences of stigma for the self-esteem of people with mental illnesses. *Psychiatric Service, 66*(2), 1,621-1,626. doi:10.1176/appi.ps.52.12.1621

Long, J., Burgess-Limerick, R., & Stapleton, F. (2014). Personal consequences of work related physical discomfort: An exploratory study. *Clinical and Experimental Optometry, 97*(1), 30-35. doi:10.1111/cxo.12066

Lupien, S. P., Seery, M. D., & Almonte, J. L. (2012). Unstable high self-esteem and the eliciting conditions of self-doubt. *Journal of Experimental Social Psychology, 48*(3), 762-765. doi:10.1016/j.jesp.2012.01.009

Maas, M., Taal, E., van der Linden, S., & Boonen, A. (2009). A review of instruments to assess illness representations in patients with rheumatic diseases. *Annals of the Rheumatic Diseases, 68*(3), 305-309. doi:10.1136/ard.2008.089888

MacEachen, E., Clarke, J., Franche, R. L., & Irvin, E. (2006). Systematic review of the qualitative literature on return to work after injury. *Scandinavian Journal Of Work, Environment & Health, 32*, 257-269. doi:10.5271/sjweh.1009

MacIntosh, J. (2012). Workplace bullying influences women's engagement in the workforce. *Issues In Mental Health Nursing, 33*, 762-768. doi:10.3109/01612840.2012.708701

Magee, D. J. (2014). *Orthopedic physical assessment* (5th ed.). St. Louis, MO: Elsevier Health Sciences.

Marks, M., Herren, D. B., Vlieland, T. P. V., Simmen, B. R., Angst, F., & Goldhahn, J. (2011). Determinants of patient satisfaction after orthopedic interventions to the hand: a review of the literature. *Journal of Hand Therapy, 24*(4), 303-312. doi:10.1016/j.jht.2011.04.004

Marras, W. S., Cutlip, R. G., Burt, S. E., & Waters, T. R. (2009). National occupational research agenda (NORA): Future directions in occupational musculoskeletal disorder health research. *Science Direct, Applied Ergonomics, 40*, 15-22. doi:10.1016/j.apergo.2008.01.018

Martin, C. J. H., & Martin, C. (2010). Bully for you: Harassment and bullying in the workplace. *British Journal Of Midwifery, 18*, 25-31. doi:10.12968/bjom.2010.18.1.45812

Martin, W., & LaVan, H. (2010). Workplace bullying: A review of litigated cases. *Employee Responsibilities and Rights Journal, 22*(3), 175-194. doi:10.1007/s10672-009-9140-4

Maxwell, J., A. (2012). *Qualitative research design: An interactive approach.* Los Angeles, CA: Sage.

May, D. R., Li, C., Mencl, J., & Huang, C.-C. (2013). The ethics of meaningful work: Types and magnitude of job-related harm and the ethical decision-making process. *Journal of Business Ethics, 121*, 651-669. doi:10.1007/s10551-013-1736-9

McCormack, D., Casimir, G., Djurkovic, N., & Yang, L. (2009). Workplace bullying and intention to leave among schoolteachers in China: The mediating effect of affective commitment. *Journal of Applied Social Psychology, 39*, 2,106-2,127. doi:10.1111/j.1559-1816.2009.00518.x

McEwan, B. (2012). Managing boundaries in the Web 2.0 classroom. *Interpersonal Boundaries in Teaching and Learning, 131*, 15-28. doi:10.1002/tl.20024

McFarlane, A. C. (2013). The long-term costs of traumatic stress: Intertwined physical and psychological consequences. *World Psychiatry, 9*, 3-10. doi:10.1002/j.2051-5545.2010.tb00254.x

McKay, R., Ciocirlan, C. E., & Chung, E. (2010). Thinking strategically about workplace bullying in organizations. *Journal of Applied Management and Entrepreneurship. 15*, 73-93.

Mellin, T., & Harriss, A. (2010). Sick and tired. *Occupational Health, 62*, 24-26.

Merriam, S. B. (2009). *Qualitative research: A guide to design and implementation.* San Francisco, CA: Wiley.

Miles, M. B., & Huberman, M. A. (1994). *Qualitative data analysis.* Thousand Oaks, CA: Sage.

Mills, J., Bonner, A., & Francis, K. (2006). The development of constructivist grounded theory. *International Journal of Qualitative Methods, 5,* 1-10. Retrieved from http://ejournals.library.ualberta.ca/index.php/IJQM/article/viewFile/4402/3795

Miner-Rubino, K., & Reed, W. D. (2010). Testing a moderated mediational model of workgroup incivility: The roles of organizational trust and group regard. *Journal of Applied Social Psychology, 40,* 3,148-3,168. doi:10.1111/j.1559-1816.2010.00695.x

Miranda, H., Kangas, L. K., Heliovaara, M., Leino-Arjas, P., Haukka, E., Lira, J., & Juntura, E. V. (2009). Musculoskeletal pain at multiple sites and its effects on work. *Occupational and Environmental Medicine, 67,* 449-455. doi:10.1136/oem.2009.048249

Montes, A., Muniz, N. M., Leal-Rodriguez, A. L., & Leal-Millan, A. (2014). Workplace bullying among managers: A multifactorial perspective and understanding. *International Journal of Environmental Research and Public Health, 11,* 2,657-2,682. doi:10.3390/ijerph110302657

Morse, J. M. (2010). *Sampling in grounded theory: The Sage handbook of grounded theory.* Thousand Oaks, CA: Sage.

Mug Kang, D., Young, K. K., & Kim, J. E. (2011). Job stress and musculoskeletal diseases. *Journal of the Korean Medical Association, 54,* 851-858. doi:10.5124/jkma.2011.54.8.851

Munnell, A. (2015). *The average retirement age – An update* (Policy brief 15-4). Retrieved from http://crr.bc.edu/briefs/the-average-retirement-age-an-update/

Murad, M. S., O'Brien, L., Farnworth, L., & Chien, C. W. (2013). Health status of people with work-related musculoskeletal disorders in Return to Work programs: A Malaysian study. *Informa Healthcare. 27,* 238-255. doi:10.3109/11038128.2012.720276

Murphy, D. R., & Rosenblum, A. (2006). Return to work after two years of total disability: A case report. *Journal of Occupational Rehabilitation, 16,* 253-260. doi:10.1007/s10926-006-9017-4

Murray, J. S. (2013). Moral distress: The face of workplace bullying. *Narrative Inquiry in Bioethics, 3,* 112-114. doi:10.1353/nib.2013.0044

Nash, J., L. (2002). And the answer is…voluntary ergonomics guidelines. *Occupational Hazards, 64,* 1-3.

Netterstrom, B., Frieble, L., & Ladegaard, Y. (2013). Effects of a multidisciplinary stress treatment program on patient return to work rate and symptom reduction: Results from a randomized, wait-list controlled trial. *Psychotherapy and Psychosomatics, 82,* 177-186. doi:10.1159/000346369

Niedhammer, I., Simone, D., Degioanni, S., Drummond, A., & Pierre, P. (2010). Workplace bullying and psychotropic drug use: The mediating role of physical and mental health status. *Annuals of Occupational Hygiene, 55,* 152-163. doi:10.1093/annhyg/meq086

Nielsen, M. B., & Einarsen, S. (2012). Outcomes of exposure to workplace bullying: A meta-analytic review. *Work & Stress, 4,* 309-322. doi:10.1080/02678373.2012.734709

Nielsen, M. B., Hetland, J., Matthiesen, S. B., & Einarsen, S. (2012). Longitudinal relationships between workplace bullying and psychological distress. *Scandinavian Journal of Work, Environment, and Health, 38,* 38-46. doi:10.5271/sjweh.3178

Nixon, A. E., Mazzola, J. J., Bauer, J., Krueger, J. R., & Spector, P. E. (2011). Can work make you sick? A meta-analysis of the relationships between job stressors and physical symptoms. *Work & Stress, 25,* 1-22. doi:10.1080/02678373.2011.569175

Nordander, C., Ohlsson, K., Åkesson, I., Arvidsson, I., Balogh, I., Hansson, G. Å., . . . Skerfving, S. (2009). Risk of musculoskeletal disorders among females and males in repetitive/constrained work. *Ergonomics, 52*(10), 1,226-1,239. doi:10.1080/00140130903056071

O'Conner, A. B. (2009). Neuropathic pain. *PharmacoEconomics, 27,* 95-112. doi:10.2165/00019053-200927020-00002

Opsteegh, L., Reinders-Messelink, H. A., Schollier, D., Groothoff, J. W., Postema, K., Dijkstra, P., U., & van der Slusi, C. K. (2009). Determinants of Return to Work in patients with hand disorders and hand injuries. *Journal of Occupational Rehabilitation, 19,* 245-255. doi:10.1007/s10926-009-9181-4

O'Reilly, J., & Aquino, K. (2011). A model of third parties' morally motivated responses to mistreatment in organizations.

Academy of Management Review, 36, 526–543. doi:10.5465/ amr.2011.61031810

O'Rourke, E. (2014). *The occupational consequences of chronic pain* (Master's thesis). Retrieved from http://ulir.ul.ie/ handle/10344/3939

Organization for Economic Cooperation and Development. (2009). *Sickness, disability and work: Keeping on track in the economic downturn.* Stockholm, Sweden: Author.

Owens, K. H., & Van Ittersum, D. (2013). Writing with(out) pain: Computing injuries and the role of the body in writing activity. *Computers and Composition, 30*(2), 87-100. doi:10.1016/j. compcom.2013.03.003

Page, K. M., & Vella-Brodrick, D. A. (2009). The "what," "why" and "how" of employee well-being: A new model. *Social Indicators Research, 90*(3), 441-458. doi:10.1007/s11205-008-9270-3

Palazzo, C., Ravaud, J. F., Papelard, A., Ravaud, P., & Poiraudeau, S. (2014). The burden of musculoskeletal conditions. *PLoS One. 9,* 1-9.

Panaccio, A., & Vandenberghe, C. (2009). Perceived organizational support, organizational commitment and psychological well-being: A longitudinal study. *Journal of Vocational Behavior, 75*(2), 224-236. doi:10.1016/j.jvb.2009.06.002

Pandit, N. R. (1996). The creation of theory: A recent application of the grounded theory method. *Qualitative Report, 2*(4). Retrieved from http://www.nova.edu/ssss/QR/QR2-4/pandit.html

Parenteau, S. C., Hamilton, N. A., Wu, W., Latinis, K., Waxenberg, L. B., & Brinkmeyer, M. Y. (2011). The mediating role of secular coping strategies in the relationship between religious appraisals and adjustment to chronic pain: The middle road to Damascus. *Social Indicators Research, 104,* 407-425. doi: 10.1007/s11205-010-9751-z

Parzefall, M.-R., & Salin, D. M. (2010). Perceptions of and reactions to workplace bullying: A social exchange perspective. *Human Relations, 63*(6), 761-780. doi:10.1177/0018726709345043

Patton, M. Q. (2002). *Qualitative research and evaluation methods* (3rd ed.). Thousand Oaks, CA: Sage.

Persson, J., Bernfort, L., Wahlin, C., Oberg, B., & Ekbert, K. (2014). Costs of production loss and primary health care interventions for return-to-work of sick-listed workers in Sweden. *Informa Healthcare, 37,* 771-776. doi:10.3109/09638288.2014.941021

Physical. (2013). *Dictionary.com.* Retrieved from http://dictionary.reference.com/browse/
physical?s=t

Pomaki, G., Franche, R. L., Murray, E., Khushrushahi, N., & Lampinen, T. M. (2011). Workplace-based work disability prevention interventions for workers with common mental health conditions: A review of the literature. *Journal of Occupational Rehabilitation. 22,* 182-195. doi:10.1007/s10926-011-9338-9

Post, M., Krol, B., & Groothoff, J. W. (2005). Work-related determinants of return to work of employees on long-term sickness absence. *Journal of Disability and Rehabilitation, 27,* 481-488. doi:10.1007/s10926-011-9326-0

Pransky, G., Benjamin, K., Hill-Fotouhi, C., Fletcher, K., E., & Himmelstein, J. (2002). Occupational upper extremity conditions. A detailed analysis of work-related outcomes. *Journal of Occupational Rehabilitation, 12,* 131-138. doi:10.1023/a:1016886426612

Prime, M. S., Palmer, J., Kahn, W. S., & Goddard, N. J. (2010). Is there light at the end of the tunnel? Controversies in the diagnosis and management of carpal tunnel syndrome. *Medicine & Public Health, 5,* 354-360. doi:10.1007/s11552-010-9263-y

Pulvers, K., & Hood, A. (2013). The role of positive traits and pain catastrophizing in pain perception. *Current Pain and Headache Reports, 17,* 330-342. doi:10.1007/s11916-013-0330-2

Radat, F., & Koleck, M. (2011). Pain and depression: Cognitive and behavioral mediators of a frequent association. *Encephale, 37,* 172-179. doi: 10.1016/j.encep.2010.08.013

Ramírez-Maestre, C., Esteve, R., & López, A. E. (2012). The role of optimism and pessimism in chronic pain patients adjustment. *The Spanish Journal of Psychology, 15,* 286-94. doi:10.5209/rev_sjop.2012.v15.n1.37335

Riach, K., & Loretto, W. (2009). Identity work and the 'unemployed' worker: Age, disability and the lived experience of the older unemployed. *Work, Employment & Society. 23,* 102–19. doi:10.1177/0950017008099780

Richardson, E. J., Ness, T. J., Doleys, D. M., Banos, J. H., Cianfrini, L., & Richards, J. S. (2009). Depressive symptoms and pain evaluations among persons with chronic pain: Catastrophizing, but not pain acceptance, shows significant effects. *Pain, 147*, 147-152. doi:10.1016/j.pain.2009.08.030

Ritchie, J., Lewis, J., McNaughton Nicholls, C., & Ormston, R. (2013). *Qualitative research practice: A guide for social science students & researchers* (2nd ed.). Los Angeles, CA: Sage.

Rodriguez-Munoz, A., Baillien, E., De Witte, H., Moreno-Jimenez, B., & Pastor, J. C. (2009). Cross-lagged relationships between workplace bullying, job satisfaction and engagement: Two longitudinal studies. *Work & Stress, 23*, 225-243. doi:10.1080/02678370903227357

Roll, S. C. (2011). Relationship of ultrasonographic physiologic changes to personal factors and psychosocial stressors in the development and diagnosis of carpal tunnel syndrome (Doctoral dissertation). Retrieved from OhioLINK: http://rave.ohiolink.edu/etdc/view?acc_num=osu1305654432

Roscigno, V., Hodson, R., & Lopez, S. (2009a). Supervisory bullying, status inequalities and organizational context. *Social Forces, 87*, 1,561-1,589. doi:10.1353/sof.0.0178

Roscigno, V., Hodson, R., & Lopez, S. (2009b). Workplace incivilities: The role of interest conflicts, social closure and organizational chaos. *Work, Employment & Society, 23*, 747–773. doi:10.1177/0950017009344875

Rubin, M. (2013). Return-to-work programs: A healthy strategy gets the job done. *Safety Management Clinic*, 7-11.

Rugulies, R. (2012). Studying the effect of the psychosocial work environment on risk of ill health: Towards a more comprehensive assessment of working conditions. *Scandinavian Journal of Work Environment & Health, 38*, 187-192. doi:10.5271/sjweh.3296

Salo, P., Oksanen, T., Sivertsen, B., Hall, M., Pentti, J., Virtanen, M., . . . Kivimaki, M. (2010). Sleep disturbances as a predictor of cause-specific work disability and delayed return to work. *Sleep, 33*, 1,323-1,331. Retrieved from PubMed.gov. (PMID: 21061854)

Samnani, A.-K., & Singh, P. (2012). 20 years of workplace bullying research: A review of the antecedents and consequences of bullying in the workplace. *Aggression and Violent Behavior, 17,* 581–589. doi:10.1016/j.avb.2012.08.004

Schuhl, K., & McMahon, M. (2006). Returning to work overcoming injury and achieving success. *Risk Management, 53,* 34-39. Retrieved from http://cf.rims.org/Magazine/PrintTemplate. cfm?AID=2985

Schumann, L., Craig, W., & Rosu, A. (2014). Power Differentials in Bullying: Individuals in a Community Context. *Journal of Interpersonal Violence, 29,* 846-865. doi:10.1177 /0886260513505708

Schur, L., Krause, D., Blasi, J., & Blanck, P. (2009). Is disability disabling in all workplaces? Workplace disparities and corporate culture. *Industrial Relations, 48,* 381-410. doi:10.1111/j.1468-232x.2009.00565.x

Seitz, E. (2010). Privacy (or piracy) of medical records: HIPAA and its enforcement. *Journal of the National Medical Association, 102,* 745-748. Retrieved from http://nmanet.org/publications/ August%202010/MLS745.pdf

Selenko, E., & Batinic, B. (2013). Job insecurity and the benefits of work. *European Journal of Work and Organizational Psychology, 22,* 725-736. doi:10.1080/1359432X.2012.703376

Shaw, W. S., Robertson, M. M., Pransky, G., & McLellan, R. K. (2003). Employee perspectives on the role of supervisor to prevent workplace disability after injuries. *Journal of Occupational Rehabilitation, 13,* 129-142. doi:10.1023/A:1024997000505

Shellenbarger, T., & Stearns., P. C. (2010). From the classroom to clinical: A Family Educational Rights and Privacy Act primer for the nurse educator. *Teaching and Learning in Nursing. 5,* 164-168. doi:10.1016/j.teln.2010.05.002

Shier, M. L., & Graham, J. R. (2011). Work-related factors that impact social work practitioners' subjective well-being: Well-being in the workplace. *Journal of Social Work, 11*(4), 402-421. doi:10.1177/1468017310380486

Shiri, R., Martimo, K.-P., Miranda, H., Ketola, R., Kaila-Kangas, L., Liira, H., . . . Viikari-Juntura, E. (2011). The effect of workplace intervention on pain and sickness absence caused by upper-extremity musculoskeletal disorders. *Scandinavian Journal* of Work, *Environment & Health, 37,* 120-128. doi:10.5271/sjweh.3141

Shoss, M. K., & Shoss, B. L. (2012). Check-up time: A closer look at physical symptoms in occupational health research. *Stress & Health: Journal of the International Society for the Investigation Of Stress, 28,* 193-201. doi:10.1002/smi.1422

Silva, F. C. M., Sampaio, R. F., Mancini, M. C., Luz, M. T., & Alcantara, M. A. (2010). A qualitative study of workers with chronic pain in Brazil and its social consequences. *Occupational Therapy International, 18,* 85-95.

Silverstein, B. A., Joyce, F. Z., Bonauto, D. K., Bao, S., Smith, C. K., Howard., N., &Viikari-Juntura, E. (2010). The natural course of carpal tunnel syndrome in a working population. *Scandinavian Journal of Work, Environment & Health,* 36, 384-393. doi:10.5271/sjweh.2912

Skakon, J., Nielsen, K., Borg, V., & Guzman, J. (2010). Are leaders' well-being, behaviors and style associated with the affective well-being of their employees? A systematic review of three decades of research. *Work & Stress, 24,* 107-139. doi:10.1080/02678373.2010.495262

Sloan, L. M., Matyiók, T., Schmitz, C. L., & Short, G. F. (2010). A story to tell: Bullying and mobbing in the workplace. *International Journal of Business and Social Science, 1,* 87-97. Retrieved from http://libres.uncg.edu/ir/uncg/f/C_Schmitz_Story_2010.pdf

Smith-Young, J., Solberg, S., & Gaudine, A. (2014). Constant negotiating: Managing work-related musculoskeletal disorders while remaining at the workplace. *Qualitative Health, 24,* 217-231. doi: 10.1177/1049732313519868

Social. (2013). *Dictionary.com.* Retrieved from http://dictionary.reference.com/browse/social?s=t

Sowislo, J. F., & Orth, U. (2013). Does low self-esteem predict depression and anxiety? A meta-analysis of longitudinal studies. *Psychological Bulletin, 139*(1), 213-228. doi:10.1037/a0028931

Spielberger, C. D., & Reheiser, E. C. (2009). Assessment of emotions: Anxiety, anger, depression, and curiosity. *Applied Psychology: Health and Well-Being, 1,* 271–302. doi:10.1111/j.1758-0854.2009.01017.x

Stahl, C., Svensson, T., Petersson, G., & Ekberg, K. (2010). A matter of trust? A study of coordination of Swedish stakeholders in Return-to-Work. *Journal Occupational Rehabilitation. 20,* 299-310. doi:10.1007/s10926-009-9205-0

Stahl, C., Toomingas, A., Aborg, C., Ekberg, K., & Kjellberg, K. (2013). Promoting occupational health interventions in early return to work by implementing financial subsidies: A Swedish case study. *BMC Public Health, 13,* 310-321. doi:10.1186/1471-2458-13-310

Stojanova, N. (2014). The regulation of workplace bullying in Victoria: Is legislation required? *Labor & Industry, 24,* 146-160. doi:10.1 080/10301763.2014.915789

Stone, S. D. (2003). Workers without work. Injured workers and well-being. *Journal of Occupational Science, 10,* 7-13. doi:10.1080/14 427591.2003.9686505

Strauss, A. L., & Corbin, J. (1998). *Basics of qualitative research: Techniques and procedures for developing grounded theory.* Newbury Park, CA: Sage.

Strunin, L., & Boden, L. I. (2000). Paths of reentry: Employment experiences of injured workers. *American Journal of Industrial Medicine, 38,* 373-384. doi:10.1002/1097-0274(200010)38:4<373::AID-AJIM2>3.0.CO;2-Y

Sullivan, M. J. L., Adams, H., & Ellis, T. (2013). A psychosocial risk-targeted intervention to reduce work disability: Development, evolution, and implementation challenges. *Psychological Injury and Law, 6,* 250-257. doi:10.1007/s12207-013-9171-x

Tang, D., Yu, I., Luo, X., Liang, Y., & He, Y. (2011). Case management after long-term absence from work in China: A case report. *Journal of Occupational Rehabilitation. 21,* 55-61. doi: 10.1007/ s10926-010-9280-2

Theberge, N., & Neumann, P. W. (2013). The relative role of safety and productivity in Canadian ergonomists' professional practices. *Département des relations industrielles, Université Laval, 68,* 387-408. doi:10.7202/1018433ar

Thomsen, N. O. B., Björk, J., & Cederlund, R. I. (2014). Health-related quality of life 5 years after carpal tunnel release among patients with diabetes: A prospective study with matched controls. *BMC Endocrine Disorders, 14,* 85-102. doi:10.1186/1472-6823-14-85

Thoits, P. A. (2013). Self, identity, stress, and mental health. In C. S. Aneshensel, J. C. Phelan, & A. Bierman (Eds.), *Handbook of the sociology of mental health* (2nd ed.; pp. 357-377). Dordrecht, Netherlands: Springer.

Tick, H. (2013). Case studies on the outcome of integrative management of Carpal Tunnel Syndrome and trigger fingers. *Global Advances in Health and Medicine, 2*, 14-85. doi:10.7453/gahmj.2013.097cp.s14c

Tinhofer, I., Draxler, R., & Koller, R. (2013). Postoperative care and rehabilitation after open carpal tunnel surgery. *European Surgery, 45*, 251-282. doi:10.1007/s10353-013-0210-3

Tracy, S. J., Lutgen-Sandvik, P., & Alberts, J. K. (2006). Nightmares, demons, and slaves: Exploring the painful metaphors of workplace bullying. *Management Communication Quarterly, 20*, 148–185. doi:10.1177/0893318906291980

Tsao, C. I. P. (2012). Chronic pain: A psychiatrist's personal illness narrative. *Academic Psychiatry, 36*, 495-496. doi:10.1176/appi.ap.12060111

Tuckey, M. R., Dollard, M. F., Hosking, P. J., & Winefield, A. H. (2009). Workplace bullying: The psychosocial work environment factors. *International Journal of Stress Management. 16*, 215-232. doi.org/10.1037/a0016841

U.S. Bureau of Labor Statistics. (2013). Nonfatal occupational injuries and illnesses requiring days away from work, 2008 [Press release]. Retrieved from http://www.bls.gov/news.release/archives/osh2_12042009.pdf

van Rijn, R. M., Huisstede, B. M., Koes, B. W., & Burdorf, A. (2009). Associations between work-related factors and the carpal tunnel syndrome: A systematic review. *ScandinavianJournal of Work, Environment & Health, 35*, 19-36. doi:10.5271/sjweh.1306

Vaught, M. S., Brismee, J., Dedrick, G. S., Sizer, P. S., & Sawyer, S. F. (2011). Association of disturbances in the thoracic outlet in subjects with carpal tunnel syndrome: A case-control study. *Journal of Hand Therapy, 24*, 44-51. doi:10.1016./j.jht.2010.09.070

Velasquez, M., G. (2006). *Business ethics concepts and cases* (6th ed.). Upper Saddle River, NJ: Pearson Prentice Hall.

Viana, S. O., Sampaio, R. F., Mancini, M. C., Parreira, V. F., & Drummond, A. (2007). Life satisfaction of workers with work-related musculoskeletal disorders in Brazil: Associations with symptoms, functional limitation and coping. *Journal of Occupation Rehabilitation, 17,* 33-46. doi: 10.1007/s10926-006-9062-z

Vie, L. T., Glasø, L., & Einarsen, S. (2010). Health outcomes and self-labeling as a victim of workplace bullying. *Journal of Psychosomatic Research. 70,* 37-43. doi:10.1016/j.jpsychores.2010.06.007

Vickers, M. H. (2009). Bullying, disability and work: A case study of workplace bullying. *Qualitative Research in Organizations and Management, 4,* 255-272. doi:10.1108/17465640911002536

Vroman, K., Warner, R., & Chamberlain, K. (2009). Now let me tell you in my own words: Narratives of acute and chronic low back pain. *Disability and Rehabilitation Journal, 31,* 976–987. doi:10.1080/09638280802378017

Wainwright, E., Wainwright, D., Keogh, E., & Eccleston, C. (2013) Return to Work with chronic pain: Employers' and employees' views. *Occupational Medicine, 10,* 501-506. doi:10.1093/occmed/kqt109

Walker, J., & Heffner, F. (2009). Explaining acquired occupational disability. *The Rehabilitation Professional, 17*(2), 51-62. Retrieved from http://www.researchgate.net/publication/239521078_Explaining_Acquired_Occupational_Disability

Walker, J. G., Jackson, H. J., & Littlejohn, G. O. (2004). Models of adjustment to chronic illness: Using the example of rheumatoid arthritis. *Clinical Psychology Review, 24,* 461-488. doi: 10.1016/j.cpr.2004.03.001

Waylett-Rendall, J., & Niemeyer, L. O. (2004). Exploratory analysis to identify factors impacting return-to-work outcomes in cases of cumulative trauma disorder. *Journal of Hand Therapy, 17,* 50-57. doi: 10.1197/j.jht.2003.10.007

Welch, L. S., Haile, E., Boden, L. I., & Hunting, K. L. (2010). Impact of musculoskeletal and medical conditions on disability retirement: A longitudinal study among construction roofers. *American Journal of Industrial Medicine, 53,* 532-560. doi:10.1002/ajim.20794

Wells, R. (2009). Why have we not solved the MSD problem? *Center of Research Expertise for the Prevention of Musculoskeletal Disorders (CRE-MSD), 34,* 117-121. doi:10.3233/WOR-2009-0937

West, C., Usher, K., Foster, K., & Stewart, L. (2011) The meaning of resilience to persons living with chronic pain: A qualitative inquiry. *Journal of Clinical Nursing, 26,* 157–176. doi:10.1111/j.1365-2702.2011.04005.x

West, C., Usher, K., Foster, K., & Stewart, L. (2012). Chronic pain and the family: The experience of the partners of people living with chronic pain. *Journal Of Clinical Nursing, 21,* 3,352-3,360. doi:10.1111/j.1365-2702.2012.04215.x

Westgaard, R. H., & Winkel, J. (2010). Occupational musculoskeletal and mental health: Significance of rationalization and opportunities to create sustainable production systems: A systematic review. *Applied Ergonomics, 42,* 261-296. doi:10.1016/j.apergo.2010.07.002

Wheeler, A. R., Halbesleben, J. R. B., & Shanine, K. (2010). Eating their cake and everyone else's cake too: Resources as the main ingredient to workplace bullying. *Business Horizons, 53,* 553-560. doi:10.1016/j.bushor.2010.06.002

Wiedmer, T. L. (2011). Workplace bullying: Costly and preventable. *Delta Kappa Gamma Bulletin, 77,* 35-41.

Workplace Bullying Institute. (2014). Impact of workplace bullying on coworkers. Retrieved from http://www.workplacebullying.org/individuals/impact/coworkers/

Wrapson, W., & Mewse, A. J. (2011). Supervisors' responses to sickness certification for an episode of low back pain: Employees' personal experiences. *Disability and Rehabilitation, 33,* 1,728-1,736. doi:10.3109/09638288.2010.544836

Wright, J. (2009). *Role stressors, co-worker support, and work engagement: A longitudinal study* (Master's thesis). Retrieved from http://scholarworks.sjsu.edu/cgi/viewcontent.cgi?article=4340&context=etd_theses

Wyatt, M. C., Jones, G., & Veale, G. A. (2013). Lamb boning: An occupational cause of carpal tunnel syndrome? *The Journal of Hand Surgery, 38,* 61-66. doi:10.1177/1753193412446885

Wynne-Jones, G., Buck, R., Porteous, C., Cooper, L., Button, L. A., Main, C. J., & Phillips, C. J. (2011). What happens to work if you're unwell? Beliefs and attitudes of managers and employees with musculoskeletal pain in a public sector setting. *Journal of Occupational Rehabilitation, 21*, 31-42. doi:10.1007/s10926-010-9251-7

Young, A. E. (2009). Return-to-work experiences: Prior to receiving vocational services. *Disability & Rehabilitation Journal, 31*, 2,013–2,022. doi:10.1080/09638280902887412

Young, W. (2009). The return of return-to-work programs. *Risk Management, 51*, 56. Retrieved from http://www.injurynet.com.au/documents/The%20Return%20of%20Return%20of%20Return-to-Work%20Programs%20-%20W%20Young%20-%20Risk%20Management%20-%20Nov%2004.pdf

APPENDIX A

Open Coding

Open Code Concept	Participant Quote	Body Language
Unwilling Acceptance	This is who I am now. I have Carpal Tunnel. (P1)	Eyes showed hurt. Entire demeanor showed defeat.
	How does that saying go, what doesn't kill you makes you stronger. Wished I believed that. (P4)	Participant looked sad. Participant moved their head a lot when speaking. Hands did not move.
Anger	They tried to break me but they can't. I've had drill sergeants try to do this and they couldn't what makes them think they can do it. (P4)	Participant's body language was cocky. Head moved back and forth when speaking. Participant had an evil grin on his face during his statement.

	Since I started in the Return to Work program my boss asks me three times a day where I am with a project. Talk about being micro managed. (P3)	Participant looked visibly shaken. Participant sat in chair but would shift from side to side. Participant kept crossing and uncrossing legs. Minimal hand gestures to emphasize statements.
Fear of the Unknown	Now what? What happens to me and my family? How do we pay the mortgage and buy food? (P2)	Obvious fear. Researcher could see the panic in the participant's eyes as they spoke. Participant's body moved forward on each statement. Hands went up as they were speaking about their checklist (mortgage and food).

Open Code Concept	Participant Quote	Body Language
Fear of the Unknown cont.	For the first time in my life I don't know if I will be able to provide for my family and that scares the hell out of me. (P4)	Participant started to look away as they were making this statement. Indicated to researcher that saying this disturbed them.
	I feel absolutely powerless against this. My own body is hurting me. (P5)	Participant would look at wrist, specifically the area where their Carpal Tunnel is as if they were looking for some indicator of where the injury exactly was. At times the participant would rub this area as well.
Medication	I started taking over the counter aspirin, which eventually increased to Ibuprofen, and now I take prescription meds. It seems like after a while I need stronger and stronger meds to make my pain go away. (P3)	Participant looked genuinely concerned about the increase in pain and taking more pain meds. Participant's voice inflections indicated they were more concerned with the pain getting worse versus having to take stronger medication.

My stomach hurts a lot from the pain meds. I try to eat before taking them, but sometimes that isn't always possible and I pay the price later with my gut aching. (P11)	Participant seemed very unfocused. Participant shifted constantly in their chair and would re adjust their seated position. Participant rarely made eye contact with the researcher directly.

Open Code Concept	Participant Quote	Body Language
Feeling Different from Co-Workers	I know I'm different now. I see the looks and the stares when I walk into a room, or when I put on my brace. I hate it. (P12)	Participant's body language reaffirmed feelings about wearing a brace and the looks from other co-workers. Participant's eyes showed anger when they said "I hate it". Researcher could feel the disgust and pain that the participant was expressing.
	I get asked a lot of questions about my injury, especially when I first came back. I feel like I am the freak show person in the circus. (P5)	Participant's body showed emotional pain. It was obvious to the researcher that the participant did not like constantly answering questions about their injury. Participant used a lot of body movements when using the term freak show.

I feel different from everyone here now because they make me feel different. For example, I have to go to the Return to Work program every day at 1:00, which means I have to stop working on what I was doing and walk over there. I once heard my co-worker sigh when I got up to leave. Do I think the two are related? You bet I do. (P2)	Participant would lean forward in the chair when speaking, but the participant never placed their hands on the table. Participant's shoulders would come forward occasionally when speaking.

Open Code Concept	Participant Quote	Body Language
Wanting to be treated like they were before	So I have an injury. Why is this such a big deal here for everyone? People get hurt. I'm no different than I was before. It takes me a bit longer to do some things, but I'm still the same person. (P9)	Participant's body language clearly indicated that they were confused about why they were being treated the way they were now. Participant's body language showed frustration by the way the participant would shift back and forth in their chair. At one point the participant grabbed the chair arms and stood up when saying they were the same person. The participant is very passionate about wanting to be treated liked they used to be.
	If everyone keeps treating me differently, then management is going to treat me differently. This is going to cost me my job. (P12)	Participant's body language showed they were frustrated and felt helpless. Participant used a lot of hand movements when speaking about management and losing their job. Participant's voice went up in pitch when they said; this is going to cost me my job. This indicates that the participant is very concerned and troubled about this.

Open Code Concept	Participant Quote	Body Language
Physical Limitations	I can't do some of the things I liked to anymore. I used to bowl, and I was really good at it. Now I can't hold a ball anymore. I tried wearing my brace to bowl, but that was painful. I got as far as swinging my arm back and I dropped the ball. (P3)	Participant held up their right hand when discussing not being able to hold a ball and made the bowling motion when talking about wearing a brace in order to show what it was like.
	Any power tools that vibrate I can't use anymore. This means I have to manually shovel snow and use one of those old lawn mowers with the blades and a bag like my grandfather used. It takes me twice as long to do these things now. (P7)	Participant looked frustrated and defeated. Participant looked very tired.

I can be in the middle of doing something and my fingers go cold and numb. I have to stop doing what I was doing and stretch. This gets so frustrating. (P10)

Participant showed the different stretches they do when talking about having to stop and stretch. Participant did not look happy doing them. Participant's body language indicated they were just going through the motions as they demonstrated their stretches.

I have a hard time typing and I code for a living. We are judged by how much code we produce in a day. I'm having a really hard time keeping up now. (P7)

Participant had a pleading look on their face when they talked about having a hard time keeping up at work. It was obvious their decreased productivity was bothering them both physically and mentally.

Open Code Concept	Participant Quote	Body Language
Physical Limitations, cont.	I can't brush my hair. I have to use my other hand. Do you have any idea how hard this is? I've had to use my left hand to eat and drink, too. I'm right handed. I feel like I am five years old and having to learn to do everything all over again. Don't they get how hard this is for me? (P9)	Participant had hands stretched out on the table and extended them outward when making statements. Participant held up right hand to emphasize they were right handed. Participant looked at right hand with disgust during the interview. Participant's inflections got quite high at times when the participant was upset.
Envy	Ever look at someone and say to yourself, I remember being able to do that? (P3) I hear my co-worker typing on the other side of the cube and I remember when I could type like that. (P9)	Participant glanced off a lot when talking about the past. It seemed that the participant was trying to feel what they once felt. Participant had a despondent look about them as they talked about what they used to be able to do. The participant seemed saddened by their limitations.

Life without carpal. Yeah, I remember that. It was nice. I miss it. (P1)	Participant's face looked as if they were grieving. At one point the participant stared past the researcher and smiled when they spoke about past life.

Open Code Concept	Participant Quote	Body Language
Blame	It's my boss's fault this happened to me. He doesn't care if I'm crippled. All he cares about is his job and making his damn stupid budget. (P4)	Participant's voice was very loud at times. Participant would point finger when talking about employer and shook it violently when talking about their employer's budget.
	If I had better computer equipment this wouldn't have happened to me. Why is my company so cheap? If they had bought me better stuff then I wouldn't be going through this. (P3)	Participant used hand gestures when stating their employer was cheap. Participant shook their head at times in disbelief when they called their company cheap.
	So now I'm crippled and this is my fault? I don't think so. If it wasn't managed chaos here and I didn't have to work so much overtime then this wouldn't have happened to begin with. (P4)	Participant leaned forward in their chair throughout interview and gripped the chair arms tightly. Participant's eyes showed anger and hate.

Self-loathing	Remember that character who always ran around saying we're doomed, we're doomed? That's how I feel, doomed. (P7)	Participant sat slouched down in chair. Participant held on to the chair arms, but not tightly. Participant did not let go of the chair arms throughout the entire interview.
	I can't do anything anymore. I chose this career and in the blink of an eye it's all over. (P11)	Participant looked out the window a lot during the interview and when speaking about their injury. Participant made minimal eye contact with researcher and looked at the floor a lot too when speaking.

Open Code Concept	Participant Quote	Body Language
Self-loathing, cont.	I can't sleep. I used to be able to sleep; now I just lay in bed looking at the ceiling and listening to the clock tick. It reminds me of my life, tick, tock, up, down, up, down. (P1)	Participant rubbed their neck a lot during the interview and occasionally their eyes. Participant's hands moved from their thighs to the chair arms back to their thighs.
Anxiety	I'm going to lose everything I worked for. My wife is going to leave me for sure. (P12)	Participant had their head back when they made this statement and was clinging to the arms of the chair.
	They are all out to get me here at work. My manager says they are hiring another person for our department, but I know this is my replacement. (P5)	Participant sat on the edge of their chair during the entire interview. Participant hit the chair arm with left hand when saying; they are all out to get me here.
	Whenever my manager talks to my co-worker in her cube, I turn my headphones off. I know they are talking about me. (P6)	Participant sat partially in chair, but leaned forward continuously onto the table and would whisper at times when talking.

	I started looking at different job boards for a new job. I know they are going to can me; it's just a matter of time, and I'm going to beat them to it. (P12)	Participant sat casually in chair and appeared cocky; legs crossed, smirking, and cupping chin with first two fingers when speaking.
Depression	I don't want to get up in the morning and I don't want to go to sleep at night. Why can't everyone and everything just go away. (P3)	Participant looked down at the table when this statement was made. Participant closed their eyes, shook their head, and held their head in their hands.

Open Code Concept	Participant Quote	Body Language
Depression, cont.	I call in sick a lot now and spend hours working out. My husband said to me, you're in the basement a lot now. I told him to mind his own business. (P9) I watch a lot of late night TV now. I used to think it was because I couldn't sleep. Now I know it's because I just don't care anymore about stuff. (P4)	Participant's body language appeared indignant as if they were trying to justify their behavior. Participant put their hands on their hips when speaking and would cock their head up. Participant put their head down when making this statement. Participant shook their head back and forth when saying they did not care anymore. Participant's eyes looked sad when saying this.
Physical Pain	I can't go to the bathroom. I didn't notice this at first, but then my clothes stopped fitting me in the waist. I thought I was just putting on weight, so I started working out more, but now my stomach hurts and is extended and bloated. (P6)	Participant looked very concerned about their health. Participant put their hands on their stomach repeatedly during interview and would leave them there for several minutes at a time.

My whole body hurts. I ache all over and the pain pills don't stop the pain. (P9)

Participant moved around a lot in their chair, turned their neck from side to side and then up and down. Participant rubbed their arms, shoulders, and thighs during interview consistently. Participant made minimal eye contact with researcher.

Open Code Concept	Participant Quote	Body Language
Physical Pain, cont.	I can't go to the bathroom, so I don't eat. I figured what's the use, why bother. At least this way I can explain what's going on inside of my body, or lack thereof. (P3)	Participant sat slouched in the chair with their legs up on the chair, curled up to their stomach. Participant would repeatedly put their head on their knees when speaking. Participant had a very hard time sitting still during the interview.
Coping Strategies	I don't say a word about my disease. If I don't talk about it, then to me it isn't as bad as it may feel sometimes. (P7)	Participant had tears in their eyes when they said this statement.
	I meditate. (P10)	Participant looked at peace when making this statement. Participant had a genuine smile on their face.

I work out. I do P90X and Insanity. This gets every bit of frustration about my day out of my body. I used to get angry, but that didn't really do me any good. At least this way I have some control over my life again and I'm OK with that. It took me a while to get here. (P8)

Participant used hand gestures when speaking and seemed comfortable talking about their coping strategies. Participant's body also seemed comfortable and relaxed in their chair. Participant sat with their legs crossed and their right leg was aimed towards the researcher.

Open Code Concept	Participant Quote	Body Language
Denial	I keep to myself. I wear my brace; I do my stretches, take my meds, and take breaks so I am not constantly at my computer. I keep thinking if I do this, then I can beat this disease and have my normal life back again. (P3)	Participant used a lot of hand movements when speaking. When the participant referred to having their normal life back again, the participant place their hands in a prayer motion as if they were pleading for this to be true.
	The pain meds make me forget that I have this and all is well. (P11)	Participant took a deep breath after making this statement. Participant then closed their eyes and rubbed their eyes before opening them and continuing with the interview.

| Loss of Self-esteem | I find myself questioning everyone and everything around me. One of my co-workers told me to get some self-confidence. Kind of hard when about a gazillion thoughts go through your head everyday about work and life and what you stand to lose because of this. (P4) | Participant sat back in the chair the entire time they were speaking. The participant rubbed top of their thighs a lot when speaking. Participant also wrung their hands a lot when speaking. |
| | I think I check my work about 50 times a day now because my manager told me I needed to be more careful and she didn't want to be my QA. Nothing like getting a review back from your manager who tells you this all the time. (P2) | Participant sat with one leg in the chair and one leg on the floor. Participant would cup the one leg in the chair with their hands. On two separate occasions, the participant placed their chin on their knee when speaking. |

Open Code Concept	Participant Quote	Body Language
Loss of Self-esteem, cont.	This brace constantly reminds me of what happened to me. I feel like a freak! I have to wear it at work; I have to wear it when I sleep. I'm constantly reminded that I'm a freak. (P5)	Participant wore their brace at the start of the interview. On the second instance when the participant described them self as a freak, the participant aggressively took their brace off with their other hand and threw it on the floor. The participant excused them self from the interview. The participant did return and was much calmer after throughout the interview. The participant did not pick up their brace until the end of the interview.
	I dropped out of school. I figured what's the point now going into debt; I don't have a future here anymore. (P6)	Participants shrugged their shoulders up and down and sometimes forward but it was not the full range of motion shrugging. Participant looked down a lot during the interview. Participant never smiled during the interview.

| Loss of Self-worth | I think the hardest part about all of this is I can't do what I used to do and every time I try, my body reminds me I can't; this really takes a toll on you after a while, you know what I mean. (P12) | Participant sat in the middle part of their chair. The participant did not change their position in their chair, but did shift their feet a lot during the interview and shook their head. Participant would glance at their hand during the interview frequently. |

Open Code Concept	Participant Quote	Body Language
Loss of Self-worth, cont.	I feel totally vulnerable now. I never felt like this before. It's like holy cow, something can hurt me and it was me that hurt me. How messed up is that! (P1)	Participant sat forward in their chair and would open and shut their right hand continuously throughout the interview. Participant shook their head back and forth when speaking, but did make eye contact with the researcher when speaking. Participant also placed their hand on the back of their neck when speaking and would rub it frequently.
Feelings about their Future and their Career	There are days when my CTS hurts so bad that I hide in the bathroom stretching until the pain subsides. I keep thinking my career is over. (P10)	Participant did make eye contact with the researcher during the interview, but when this statement was made, the participant looked away as if the participant was ashamed to say this.

I had a future once, but now that is gone. My boss e-mails me asking for status reports on my projects at least twice a week. I asked my co-worker if she has to do this and she says she doesn't. You can't tell me my days aren't numbered here. (P8)

Participant sat straight in their chair during the entire interview. Hands were not visible however. Participant made purposeful that they wanted to make eye contact with the researcher.

Open Code Concept	Participant Quote	Body Language
Feelings about their Future and their Career, cont.	Future? What future? I have Carpal Tunnel Syndrome. There's no cure for this. I use my hands for a living. Now I won't be able to even push a stupid broom. Yeah, I have a real bright future. Doing what, I haven't the slightest clue! (P1)	Participant used a lot of hand gestures and threw their hands up in the air when saying what future. Participant also looked up at the ceiling when saying I haven't the slightest clue.
Feelings about CTS	I hate this disease and what it did to my life! (P7)	Participant's eyes flared and stared directly at the researcher when asked about their feelings about CTS. Participant's mouth tightened talking about the disease.
	My life is ruined! (P12)	Participant held their head when making this statement. Participant shook their head and rocked back and forth in their chair.
	This is the worst thing that could have happened to me. Every, everything is changed now. (P11)	Participant took a deep breath before making this statement and then looked away after saying it. Participant looked back at researcher and it appear as if they were trying to look through the researcher.

Appendix B

Sociological Overcompensation

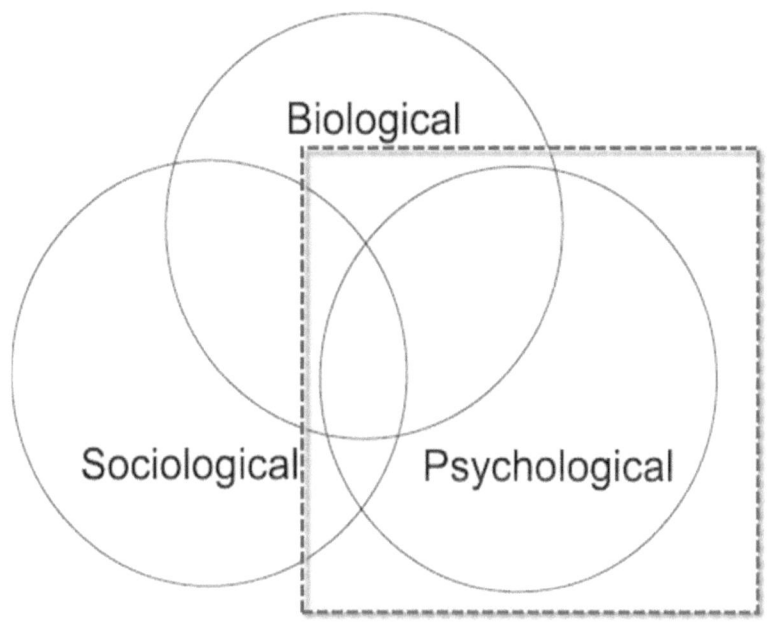

-----, Indicates Removed.

SmartDraw Academic Edition

Appendix C

Left With No Way To Cope With Symptoms

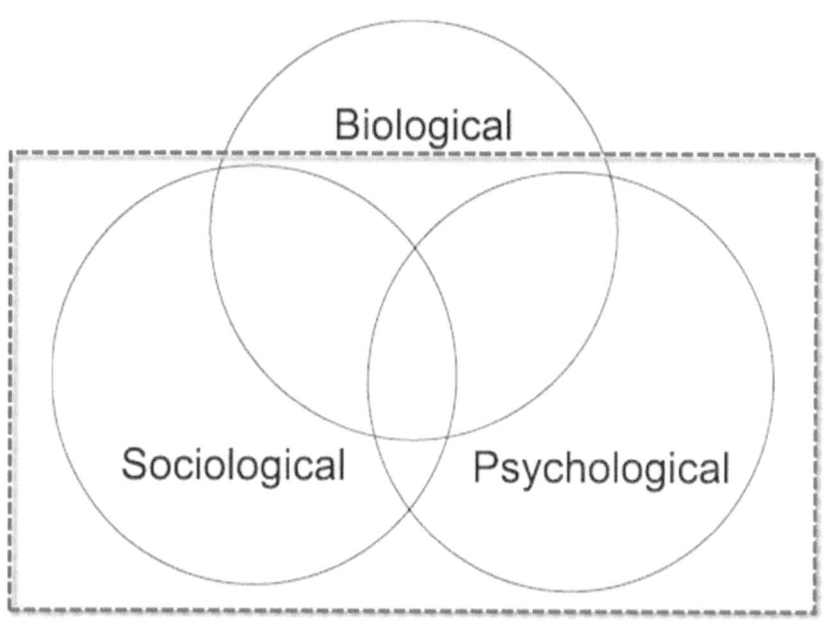

- - - - Indicates Removed.

SmartDraw Academic Edition

ABOUT THE AUTHOR

My story begins the day I got hurt at work. That's when my life changed. In 2005, I was diagnosed with carpal tunnel syndrome, and within a week of reporting my injury to my manager, I was fired from my position. According to the human resources department, "You are no longer capable of doing the job you were hired to do." It took me three months to find another job, and I used workers' compensation as a means to pay for the medical bills associated with my injury.

Interestingly enough, my life was changed by a complete stranger with these words during my electromyogram: "Is there anything else you can do with your life?" These words echoed in my head and became my crucible. I never forgot that nurse, and while I spent the next two years fighting the insurance company for my medical bills, which totaled many thousands of dollars, to be paid, I never forgot that question, and I vowed no one would ever go through what I did again.

Eventually I did find work, but the first day at my new job, I hesitated to put on my brace, fearful of quickly being let go. When asked why I was wearing it, I lied, saying it was preventative maintenance. To add legitimacy to my statement, I added some medical terminologies to explain my rationale, and once I saw the person was very confused by what I was saying, I knew they would not ask me again. Before seeking alternative medical treatments for my carpal tunnel syndrome symptoms in 2009, this was my life.

I'm ecstatic to say that the alternative medical treatment gave me my freedom back. Through the use of stretching techniques, I could once again use my right wrist and not wear a brace, nor have I since 2009.

This part of my experience with this disease made me even more determined to examine ways to help people. In the 2015 winter semester at Capella University, I completed my doctoral study, which examined why employees with carpal tunnel syndrome do or do not complete their employer-sponsored return-to-work program. I did this through the use of a constructivist grounded theory approach, which utilized semistructured interviews, open-ended interviews, and observations in order to learn about the essence of this disease. The experience I had with interviewing my participants was amazing. Each one came into my study with a story to tell, and when they left, I was and I am a better doctor for knowing them.

I do not believe my work with this disease is finished. As a matter of fact, I believe it is only the beginning. However, if I have learned anything from this experience, I have learned in order to effectively treat any disease, you have to treat the human aspect of the disease if you want to help the person heal.

www.ingramcontent.com/pod-product-compliance
Lightning Source LLC
Chambersburg PA
CBHW030446290526

45786CB00001B/468